OPEN LETTER TO PRESIDENT DONALD TRUMP

OPEN LETTER TO PRESIDENT DONALD TRUMP

STEL MIHUT

CONTENTS

INTRODUCTION

You're living a lie. We're all living a lie, and the sad truth is, America – our country, our home that we love – is dying by "The Death of a Thousand Cuts."

The violent acts mercilessly inflicted upon us; how the American people and their children are killed every year in acts of violence that the Democrats openly welcome through the borders of this great nation; the massive corruption going on inside our own government; all the illegal immigrations, crimes, drugs, terrorism; all of this has to stop.

It's time to stand up, speak out, and let your voice be heard. It's time to uncover the truth, ignite change, and begin shaping a future for a better nation, a nation that is OURS, not theirs. So, the real question is: Are you ready to take action and save our country?

This political commentary is a wake-up call for all American patriots. From economic instability to social unrest, it provides practical solutions to help address our country's greatest fears and aims – through insightful analysis and bold recommendations – to wake up America to the harsh realities that we face.

The author – a poor immigrant himself – came to America with nothing but a suitcase and a dream: the American dream of freedom and honor; a dream of a place where democracy reigned supreme and the government was made for the people, by the people. And for a while it was… until – slowly and unnoticed at first – communists and democracy haters slithered their way into our government, slowly poisoning it and destroying what people like George Washington strove so hard to build. So, nine years ago, the author decided to write this book for all the American people, hoping to open their eyes and make them realize how much damage was done to the USA by the Enemy Within.

While it's true America is at a very low point right now, stripped of its former glory and left crippled for the predators of the world, it's NOT dead yet.

We can still come together; it is our DUTY as real American Patriots to come together, no matter race or religion or political party, and take a stand for our beloved home. Only by speaking out and taking action together can we ensure that America remains a beacon of hope and liberty for generations to come.

The first step in Making America Great Again is choosing a leader that truly loves our country and is ready to fight to the death to restore its greatness.

So, Patriots, let us unite and Revolt by Vote to make sure the great United States of America get the president it deserves: Donald Trump 2024.

Come on, Mr. President, our home, our future, the American dream depends on you, and we are all pulling for your success.
Let's drill America out of fear, darkness, and indifference together, because United we stand stronger than ever!
Revolt by Vote!
MAGA!

PRESIDENT TRUMP

**President Donald Trump is the perfect example of the
adage:**
"That Which Doesn't Kill You, Makes You Stronger"
He is getting stronger than ever and American citizens see
that and love it.
**President Donald Trump: The George Washington of
Today**
Will lead us to the dawn of a new, better, stronger United
States of America.

Our predecessors built a phenomenal country and the best
Constitution ever, just as good today as it was when first
signed on March 4, 1789.

The most important and powerful country in the history of
the world. But in the last 50-60 years, we let our guard

down and allowed the Communists and the American haters to hijack our educational system, from K to 12, the colleges, the universities, most government jobs and departments including the FBI, CIA, DOJ, the State Department, and so many others. Most government jobs are infested with this kind of American haters and Communists, who want to see this country turn into a tyrannical system. They make tons of money, work no more than a few hours a week (mostly plotting against the USA), and enjoy huge benefits and retirement with more than twice their salaries, mind you, after only 25 years of employment (NOTE I did not say 25 years of work). How is that right? How is that even possible?

President Trump and the conservatives should try to unite all Americans by better explaining what America is all about, what we stand for, what capitalism is, and what socialism/communism is not. **IS NOT.**

First, let's apologize to the citizens of this great country for the fact that Congress and Presidents lost their way and focus over the last 50-60 years. They allowed these American haters and Communists to infiltrate, slowly, into all of these important government jobs, from where they could change our American way of life. Both Houses of Congress and Presidents have also forgotten that they are working for us, for the American people, not the other way around. After all, they are public servants. Or did they forget this?

They should all take the example of President Donald Trump. During his first term, he worked for a $1.00 per year salary. The rest went to charities. That is truly a public servant. But not just a public servant, but a patriot like no other. He loves this country very much, and he took this job knowing very well that he would be attacked from all sides: Republicans, Democrats, and the Fake News Media. In both Houses of Congress, politicians, are supposed to be public servants. Unfortunately, they are far from that. On the contrary, they are self-servants. They are just using us and think we are all stupid for believing in their lies year after year, and because of it, we deserve to work for them. Just a few of them are true patriots and public servants.

Republicans have to explain to the American people better, in layman's words, so everybody will get it and explain in all kinds of venues, to reach as many people across the USA as possible. Explain to them that socialism/communism is nothing like what the communism sympathizers preach it to be. That everybody in communism is equal—yes, they are equal, equally poor, except for their elite. That everybody in a communist country is a prisoner of the state. That the communist country is nothing but a big prison, where you are not free to speak or have an opinion about anything, especially the party in power. Period. In other words, you are a prisoner/slave of the state. Look at North Korea, a perfect example. No one in, no one out. And no, China and Russia are not communist regimes anymore, they are dictatorships. Not much better than communists unless you are one of the elites, and yes, you may travel to other countries if you can afford to.

Once President Trump is elected again and the country prospers big time, following the first two years of success and proving to the American people that President Donald Trump and the Republicans are doing a great job, I think that maybe President Trump should entertain the idea of setting up a new major political party—the MAGA Party (people who believe that the America First concept is the right priority).

I think that we should involve the best of all the party platforms—Republican, Democratic, Independent, and Libertarian—and make the MAGA Party platform even better than all of them put together, completed with something that no one else ever had before caveat as follows:

Every member of the MAGA Party is to sign a contract with the MAGA Party (and indirectly with the American people) that they will do just as promised in their MAGA Charter and that if caught in a lie or do not live up to what they promised on the campaign trail, they will not be able to run again in the next election cycle, or ever. We will have to show the American people that we mean business, that you, MAGA members, are committed to the truth and the American people, that you say what you mean and mean what you say.

• They will pass a law that all politicians can only serve for two 4-year terms. No exceptions. This will attract the best people from all political spectrums and walks of life to enter the political arena. Good for the country

• Together, we will make the USA a true democracy like no other.

• The USA will be again the envy of all the countries in the world.

• We will give the opportunity to everybody who is in the USA legally to shine in whatever endeavor they engage in.

• We will rebuild America within 10 years to the level that will make every single one of us proud again to be an American. Put out a plan and show it to the whole country.

• We will not have homeless people in America anymore.

• Education will make us number one in the whole world, bar none.

• America must be energy self-sufficient. We must not ever let other countries be able to control our destiny. First, as Mr. Trump said, "Drill, baby, drill."

- They will bring all manufacturing back to America; at least 75% of everything we need has to be made in America.

- The gangs will be a thing of the past, making laws so tough they will take their business someplace else. Meanwhile, we will arrest and deport every one of these gangsters to their country of origin.

- Many other things can be added to this list, for sure.

- Balance the budget within 6 years. It is not impossible.

- Plan how to pay back the trillions of dollars we owe in the next 15-20 years. Yes, this is doable. We have lots of oil and natural gas. President Donald Trump has the answer again: "Drill, baby, drill."

Benjamin Franklin, one of our Founding Fathers, was also an author, politician, civic activist, diplomat, scientist, and more. Anyway, listen to what he said:

PAY ATTENTION and don't EVER forget it:

"They that can give up essential liberty to obtain a little temporary safety deserve neither liberty nor safety."

We MUST restore our liberty that we lost after 9/11, we MUST.

With GOD'S help through President Donald Trump, we will clean up our country, which is full of Communists and

America haters. We are going to be the best ever, a country where everybody wants to be, where everyone is proud to work, and where there will be lots of jobs in all kinds of fields. NOT GOVERNMENT JOBS. No, these people will be looking for work. American people will be respected again. No more homelessness. Very little crime.

A country where everybody is going to want to work, get involved, and be part of this great democracy. It is a wonderful feeling to work, to be productive, to know that you are in control of your own destiny. It's empowering. I should know this; I have been working since I was just 15 years old, and I will still love to work long after I retire.

I hope that Donald Trump will help to form a commission with the best evangelists in America. Have them organize religious crusades in all the states, all the while he is president and after. The type of crusades the great Billy Graham used to have. His son, Franklin Graham, knows what I am talking about. Guide the American people and share with them the good news. Bring back the young people to Christ and teach them the values of families again. Hopefully, this will bring back life the way it used to be in the '50s, '60s, and '70s. It was, for me, the best time that life had to offer. Almost everybody I knew in those days was happy people, happy families.

It took 50-60 years for the prior administrations to allow the Communists and America haters to infiltrate this great nation in all the right places, yes, even infiltrate both Houses of Congress and even the Presidency. From there, they constantly and methodically changed the way our children think and how they look at this beautiful country of ours. They even tried to rewrite our history and took down some of our monuments. Shame on us for letting them get away with that. We should restore every one of them. It's time to identify these people and expose them to the American people. Make sure that these people can NEVER be elected or hired for any job of any importance. Maybe a dog catcher. Maybe.

I hope that President Donald Trump, in the first six months, will begin a major unwind of all the prior traitorous issues that President Biden brought us.

We owe President Donald Trump a sincere debt of gratitude for what he did for this country in his first term. I pray that he will have a lot more support and strength to do what is right for our great nation in his second term. Now that he knows who the snakes are, I hope he will stay away from them. Most of them revealed themselves in the last four years. The likes of Nikki Haley, Chris Christie, William Barr, Mitt Romney, Mike Pence, and others. The list is long. What phony human beings. President Donald Trump helped every one of these self-serving sorry excuses for politicians. How do they look at themselves in the mirror? How do they sleep at night? How do they explain their behavior to their kids?

On uniting the country

I just wish Donald Trump would try to set up monthly breakfast/prayer meetings with some of the Democrats, Independents, and Libertarians, but ONLY the ones that we know love America, the patriots who want what's good for America, the ones that we know who they are. Bring them to the table and talk, form a coalition with all the great ones we have in Congress and the Senate, but ONLY the ones that he is sure are trying to help bring the country together. Get them involved in the process and plan for America's bright and wonderful future. DO NOT allow the likes of Elizabeth Warren, Bob Menendez, Cory Booker, Chuck Schumer, Mitt Romney, Bernie Sanders, Eric Swalwell, Adam Schiff, Maxine Waters, Jerrold Nadler, and especially NOT Nancy Pelosi. The list goes on. They are just a few of the American haters. So many more of these people who hate our way of life—it is just hard for me to believe these people were born in America. They would rather have TYRANNY than democracy. DON'T let them in. Please keep this up throughout your presidency.

Also, campaign heavily for all the good and young Republicans to be elected to both houses of Congress. Having control of the Senate and Congress, we will keep moving forward as fast as possible to better the American way.

I think President Donald Trump should NOT leave it to chance in our next presidential election in 2028 and start to prepare someone or even two great patriots that he thinks are going to continue with the work of Making America Great Again.

President Trump MUST surround himself only with people who love America and love the American Constitution. It's OUR responsibility, ALL of the American citizens, that on November 5th, we MUST go out and VOTE and start early, bring a friend or two. Save America from TYRANNY, make a difference, and elect the people who truly love America and love the American way of life. And love our great Constitution.

We MUST always remember what Aesop said: **"UNITED WE STAND, DIVIDED WE FALL."**

In this great country of ours, we, the people, WANT equal opportunity to do whatever job we desire, as long as we have the qualification for it.

I think that natural-born citizens should be the first choice, if qualified. Then the naturalized American citizens, and then green card holders. Never the illegals, for any job whatsoever. I think that is only fair to the American citizens born here, educated here, and who have lived here all their lives and, if qualified, to get a crack at the job. I am an American citizen and very proud to be able to say that, but I was not born here. I believe that we should all have to earn our way to the top. I also believe in equal pay for equal work no matter who you are or what color you are.

So yes, we are all God's people and we all have the same exact rights. All of us. No matter what color, no matter what shape, no matter what gender or religion. We also have the right to make decisions for ourselves and our families, what we want to do, how hard we want to work, or how much we do not want to work.

Winston Churchill said in a speech, **"We shall never surrender, never give in."** Let this be our new American motto: "We will never surrender to the terrorists; we will never throw in the towel to the American haters and the communists who pretend to be patriots." NEVER.

President Donald Trump is an amazing human being. I can't think of any other man on this earth who could have accomplished everything he has done and put up with so much hate from the left and even from his own party. Here are just a few of President Donald Trump's accomplishments during his first term in office, not all, not by a long shot:

1. Supreme Court Judges Neil Gorsuch, Brett Kavanaugh, and Amy Coney Barrett

2. Took us out of TPP

3. Illegal immigration was down 70% (the lowest in 17 years)

4. Arranged for a 7% to 24% tariff on lumber from Canada

5. Started to build the wall he promised, approximately 400 miles

6. Pulled out of the lopsided Paris Accord

7. Keystone pipeline approved

8. NATO allies boosted spending by 4.3%

9. Allowed VA to terminate bad employees

10. Allowed private healthcare choices for veterans

11. Created more than 600,000 jobs

12. Median household income at a 7-year high

13. China agreed to American import of beef and $89 billion was saved in regulation rollbacks

14. MOAB for ISIS

15. Travel ban reinstated

16. Executive order for religious freedom

17. Jump-started NASA

18. $600 million cut from the UN peacekeeping budget

19. Targeting MS13 gangs

20. Deporting violent illegal immigrants

21. Trump economy took over 7,000,000 people off food stamps

22. Created a commission on voter fraud

23. Achieved 40 months in a row with more job openings than hirings

24. Gave power to states to drug test unemployment recipients

25. Unemployment lowest since May 2007

26. Historic Black College University initiative

27. Women in Entrepreneurship Act

28. Reversed Dodd-Frank

29. Ended DAPA program

30. Stopped companies from moving out of America

31. Promoted businesses to create American jobs

32. Encouraged big companies to bring their business back to America

33. Cut regulations – 2 for every one created

34. Reviewed all trade agreements to make sure they are America first

35. Highest manufacturing surge in 3 years

36. $78 billion promised reinvestment from major businesses like Exxon, Bayer, Apple, SoftBank, and Toyota

37. Denied FBI a new building

38. $700 million saved with F-35 renegotiation

39. Saved $22 million by reducing White House payroll

40. Treasury reports a $182 billion surplus for April 2017 (2nd largest in history)

41. Gas prices lowest in more than 12 years

42. Signed an executive order to promote energy independence and economic growth

43. Worked with Congress to pass more legislation in his first 100 days than any president since Truman

44. Unemployment rate down to 3.5% – the lowest in 50 years

45. Refused his presidential paycheck

46. Middle-class family income increased by approximately $6,000.00

47. Jobless claims were at a 50-year low

48. African American homeownership rose by 41%

49. DOW grew from below 20,000 in 2016 and topped over 30,000 in 2020

Wow, that is absolutely astounding. Just think of these facts. There are so many things he has done for the American people. And these are just a few of his great accomplishments. There are probably hundreds more, but I want this to be easy reading.

And another thought to Mr. Donald Trump: Thomas Friedman said, ***"The country that owns green, that dominates the industry, is going to have the most energy security, economic security, competitive companies, healthy population, and most of all, global respect."***

GLOBAL RESPECT

THE THREAT TO US SECURITY

1. One of the biggest threats to US security is the liberal news media. Yes, they are the Enemy Within. The lies and propaganda that they use on us and our young future generation are heinous. It is CRIMINAL, nothing less. How can they be allowed to get away with these continuous loathsome lies and propaganda, year after year, on the American people? WHY does no one in Congress stand up and raise this issue and put a stop to it? Where is the FCC?

The reason they hate President Donald Trump and his supporters so much is because he is undoing everything the Communists and the American haters have been doing for the last 50-60 years - destroying the American way of life, history, and family values. President Donald Trump just wants to bring back the America that we knew and loved so much for so many decades, where everyone had a chance at the American Dream. Everyone, NO exceptions.

2. Another huge threat to the safety and security of the United States is the illegal immigrants that are pouring into the United States by the millions every year through the State of Mexico. Some are hardened criminals, murderers, child molesters, mentally sick people, spies from everywhere, especially CHINA, our biggest ENEMY, sick people that spread diseases to our population (like tuberculosis, hepatitis, and many other diseases that Americans hadn't had in over 60 years), and not least, terrorists. We all know how much they love us (being sarcastic).

This is totally unacceptable in today's administration, and they should be held responsible and liable for all the future crimes that the illegal immigrants have been inflicting on the American people and all the damages done to the US.

3. CHINA - We were so stupid that we helped them become what they are today. They ARE without a doubt our greatest ENEMY today. Instead of thanking us for helping them develop into such an industrious country and letting them steal from the USA technology worth billions of dollars, Xi Jinping is hell-bent on destroying our way of life. They say if you don't let somebody die, he won't let you live. So true. He has been planning to first destroy our manufacturing. In the meantime, he sent hundreds, if not thousands, of spies

working for our Congressmen and Senators, maybe even the White House. Many of their engineers/spies are getting jobs with research and innovation companies, STEALING our best inventions, IT, and AI technologies. They sent young smart kids to attend our best universities, paying lots of money and taking the places of our AMERICAN kids. It is CRIMINAL for these universities to take money from China, which wants to destroy us.

4. RUSSIA - Just waiting in the wings, praying that we make a mistake, like Joe Biden, and then hitting whoever they want. Not only that but now they have signed some kind of agreement with China to help each other in case of an attack. FROM WHOM? I ask you. Nobody was ever going to attack either one of them. Except maybe each other.

IRAN - This government is a TERRORIST government. No questions there. They have been trying to build a nuclear bomb for years with the help of North Korea and maybe even Russia. I wonder why. Not for the sake of peace, that's for sure. They want to destroy ISRAEL, and that is just the beginning. Iran's neighbors are NOT safe either. They will be next on their list. Iran has many enemies in the area. If left alone, next they will think they can attack the USA. We can NEVER allow them to build the nuclear bomb. We can never allow them to even think they can take out Israel.

5. IRAN - This Government is a **terrorist** Government. No questions there. They have been trying to build a **nuclear**

bomb for years now. With the help of North Korea and maybe even Russia. I wonder why? Not for the sake of peace, that is for sure. NO. First and foremost, they want to destroy Israel and that would be just the beginning. Iran over the years has made many enemies in the area. So Iran hates most of its neighbors and won't hesitate to use it against any of them either. So they will be next on the list. It's going to be only a matter of time before they would think, why not hit America, and teach them a lesson? Yes, this is how this Mullahs thing. We can **never** afford to allow them to even come close to building a nuclear bomb. Or even think that they can take out Israel. They also finance and supply many terrorist groups throughout the area. They are a huge threat to America.

6. TERRORISM - Hamas, Hezbollah, Afghan Taliban, Houthi in Yemen, Al Shabaab in Somalia, and many others. The USA MUST work with Israel and our friends in the Arab world and make them understand that these terrorist groups, wherever they may be, MUST be OBLITERATED in the true sense of the word. If NOT, thanks to Iran, these groups WILL get better and stronger, will have more ammunition, and will be more dangerous for everybody around. NO GAMES, everybody in. They must be killed. It's for the world's good and the world's peace. Instead of wanting to live in harmony with the world and spend money to better the living conditions for their people, they spend their lives organizing and killing other innocent

people and want to kill more and more. These terrorists are not human. They are barbarians. All they do is plan how to kill more innocent people. Who does this?

Do you want to fight? Get an army to declare war on whoever you want to battle with. But these terrorists are savages hired by Iran to do their dirty work, destabilizing the whole area. They want to look good to the world, but they go about it the wrong way. But yes, the Iranians, are the ones spending billions of dollars to finance all these terrorist groups and tell them exactly what to do and when to do it.

- *"Terrorism isn't insanity. It grows out of social conditions that are well known: poverty, social oppression, dictatorship, and a void of meaning in the lives of ordinary people."* — Deepak Chopra, American author and alternative medicine advocate.

7. The MOSQUES in the USA. The mosques in the USA, where imams deliver hate speeches against the USA all the time, are a growing concern. These American haters must be arrested at once and sent back to the countries from which they came, immediately. They should never be able to return to the USA, receive no visa ever, and be placed on the no-fly list. These are hate speeches and will not be tolerated anymore. They also train future terrorists inside their mosques. Any imam recorded making such a hate speech should have the evidence used against them in a court of

law. The first plane back to where they came from is in order. Amen.

Welcoming Immigrants. People in this country we call America have welcomed tens of millions of people to its beautiful land for the last two hundred years. They were a great asset to the United States and its economy. Most of us love it here and want to keep this beautiful country just the way it has been for over two centuries. If anything, we want to make it better than what we found. But lately, **most immigrants** seem to come here just for the free money America has to offer, not necessarily caring for our country, or outright hating us and wanting to do us harm.

The Border Wall. Why are the Democrats so afraid of this wall at the border? Why don't they want to stop illegal immigrants from coming in, including terrorists, gangs, spies, and the millions of people who come to the US to live here for free, abusing the system? All these Illegals are creating chaos, killing our citizens, damaging our infrastructure, and drugs everywhere. How about all the gangs in all our Cities?

They don't want to stop this madness because all these people, in five years, will be given citizenship and vote Democratic. They vote illegally even now, all the time. The Democrats have lost voters by the millions in the past year, so they need to import new blood—people who will listen to their lies for the next 50-60 years.

The wall must be built and completed within a year. No more fooling around. It has to be guarded so even a mouse couldn't get in anymore. No illegals and no drugs.

Bring Back the American Dream

Bob Marley once said, ***"The people who were trying to make this world worse are not taking a day off. Why should I?"* We must always be vigilant.**

INFRASTRUCTURE

John Hickenlooper, American Politician: *"Infrastructure investments lead to jobs. And quality of life starts with a good job."*

Hopefully, once President Donald Trump takes office for his second term, one of the first things on his priority list should be a 10-year massive investment program in America's infrastructure throughout the country.

New train systems should be even faster and better than what China has built. (We are the United States of America after all, let's have some pride in what we are doing from now on.) This will relieve congestion on all highways and streets of all major cities, automatically reducing pollution significantly, and everybody happy, right? Red tape must be cut down in a big way. We cannot afford to wait 20-30 years to build a single highway or train track. This is totally unacceptable. We have the manpower and the technology to do it.

All public transportation must run on natural gas. Natural gas is 90% less polluting than gasoline and can be implemented right away. Changing over from gasoline to natural gas is not as expensive as some claim to be.

All semi-trucks, and any truck for that matter, must run on natural gas within one year. It is a very small cost to the operators, somewhere between $500 and $750. All new such vehicles must run on natural gas. This alone would save tons of carbon from going into the air, helping with a much better air. The extra cost per vehicle would barely increase by approximately $200.

Semi-trucks should not be allowed to drive around during peak driving hours. During the 1984 Olympics, Commissioner Peter Ueberroth coordinated with all the surrounding cities of Los Angeles to restrict semi-truck driving to between the hours of 10 p.m. and 6 a.m. Traffic during the Olympics ran better than before or after the event, even with millions of extra tourists participating during the event. There were also fewer accidents—a win-win situation. Let's do it again and make it permanent in all big cities across the country.

New bridges are needed to replace old ones, many of which are unsafe. A few old bridges have collapsed in recent years.

The power grid must be rebuilt from the ground up. It is way too old, outdated, and unsafe.

New dams, providing free and sustainable hydroelectric power, must be built. The last dam was built more than 40 years ago (Hoover Dam). We should build a new dam every 10 years to create more clean hydroelectric power, which is desperately needed. New dams also mean new large lakes, which are great for the environment by helping combat climate change and saving some rivers.

We spend billions of dollars on stupid things and foolish projects instead of investing in our future—the American future. If we don't start now, tomorrow might be too late. Get started today.

A powerful and aggressive educational system with incentives for young men and women to attend universities and become teachers or professors is essential. They should genuinely love this type of work and love to teach kids. Kids are our future and our biggest treasure. So let us invest in our kids. All charter schools should be supported everywhere. The school environment must be right, as many teachers and professors in some areas are scared to teach. Rebuild the system. For more on education, see Chapter 8 on "Education."

America is in big trouble right now. It needs huge amounts of money for infrastructure of all types. This also means new jobs and new jobs mean more taxes to pay off our crazy debt. It also means a better life and a better life means a happier America.

CONSERVATIVE INFLUENCERS

William R. Hearst said: *"A politician will do anything to keep his job, even become a PATRIOT."*

Candace Owens, Sean Hannity, Bill O'Reilly, Ben Shapiro, Charlie Kirk, Tucker Carlson, the Great One, Mark R. Levin, and so many other great Conservatives

Another thought to you comes from Henry Ford, who said, **"If everyone is moving forward together, then success takes care of itself."**

- You must all unite, get together, and pull in the same direction. Work with President Donald Trump, and help him spread the word. Why don't you get together and buy a national TV station like CBS, NBC, or ABC? These TV stations are in every corner of America. These stations now have a monopoly where cable news doesn't go. It would be good to have one of these stations to actually tell the news, not manufacture the news. Inform the people of what is going on all the time

• Use all the right social media that is available: Truth Social, "X," Telegram... One of the major points in this election is to involve the young generation. We have to convince them that this time is different than ever before. They exercise their responsibility to get involved and VOTE. We want them to get involved. We need them. THEY are the future of this country, and we want them to UNDERSTAND that. It's time for them to get involved in politics before it's too late. Let's throw out all the politicians that have been there for more than 12 years. It's time to "REVOLT BY VOTE."

• The country needs this young generation in the House of Representatives, the Senate, and all around the Federal Government. And I don't mean the kind of Alexandria Ocasio-Cortez, Ilhan Omar, Ayanna Pressley, and Rashida Tlaib. This so-called squad is American haters of the worst kind. Big American haters. Look at their record. Listen to what garbage comes out of their mouths. VOTE them OUT. They truly hate America. We want young people who LOVE America and its future. We want people who are interested in having a family and kids with a bright future ahead of them. We believe in America's bright future.

• We want to rebuild the school system from the ground up, so everyone, no matter what city or neighborhood they live in, will get the same great education everywhere. We want a great and bright future for all of our kids, and I MEAN ALL OF OUR KIDS. The government should issue vouchers for every single kid in America. That way, they all have equal opportunity.

• We are sick and tired of having lazy people, incompetent people, half-senile or in their 80s and 90s, in our CONGRESS. People who have been there for so long that they are out of touch with reality. It should ONLY be a two-term limit for everybody. *See the chapter **"Politicians"** for more information on how politicians should be elected. No money should be involved. **NO MONEY.** Help the American people right the ship.

• Talk about how to UNITE THE COUNTRY. I mean Republicans, Democrats, Libertarians, and Independents. We are all Americans. We want to engage ALL Americans to take this country back. How to influence the young generation to be good American citizens and patriots and what it means to be a good citizen and a good American.

• I think that CPAC, the Heritage Foundation, the American Enterprise Institute's World Forum, and the Federalist Society's Lawyers Convention should all get together and promote the American Dream. They are all great organizations. Unfortunately, they meet ONLY once a year.

I strongly feel that they should meet at least four times a year and in different cities every time. Get everybody all over the country to participate in such events by running heavy promotions. Discover and develop new potential members to join the conservative movement. We want to change our politicians every 4 to 8 years. We need new men and women, young people who believe in this movement and are willing to join this movement, to make the United States a better-than-ever country. Do this every year. We don't ever want the communists and American haters to get any power ever again. We want to expose who they are so people can VOTE them out. We have to be vigilant. We MUST be for the sake of our country and for the sake of our kids and future generations. We MUST vote these politicians out en masse this November 5th, 2024. They are pushing American society towards tyranny and fast. Let's get off our butts and get to work. VOTE out anybody who has been there for more than 12 years. VOTE for the young vibrant, bright, and American-loving Patriots. Time is short, and the work is hard. Let's get going. It's our time to shine and get going great American Patriots

• Help President Donald Trump Make America Great Again. MAGA all the way. You guys will go down in history as leaders of this great movement that will change the course of history. I would like to call it the American Revolution 2.0 (Intellectual Revolution). To get our country back from these tyrants who DISREGARD our great

AMERICAN CONSTITUTION and make a circus of our judicial system.

• Just look at what they've tried to do to our President Donald Trump. We can NEVER forget or forgive this. THEY ARE EVIL. If we don't get the country back, you and I are next.

Ron Paul nailed it here: *"There is nothing wrong with describing conservatism as protecting the Constitution, protecting all things that limit government. Government is the enemy of liberty. Government should be very restrained."*

SOCIAL MEDIA

George Washington once said: ***"Guard Against the Impostores of Pretended Patriotism."***

This is what we MUST protect ourselves against more than anything else. We have to watch for THE ENEMY WITHIN. Our news and social media, school system (including universities), and political system are infested with "IMPOSTERS OF PRETENDED PATRIOTISM," and we all know who they are. They are everywhere. They can be individuals or even groups that falsely claim they love their country and would do anything to prove it. But of course, they never do. The louder they are, the more the claims, the more you have to be aware of them and keep an eye on their actions. They will talk rhetorically to deceive others while advancing their agenda. Their values NEVER align with our values. Individuals who falsely try to discredit others to push their own agenda. Sounds familiar? They fuel conflicts and even threaten national security. We have to be more VIGILANT than ever. They are on our doorsteps, ready to kick our door down. Let's NOT let them do that.

Social Media, are everywhere indeed. Facebook, Instagram, YouTube, LinkedIn, Snapchat, Twitter (thank God now "X" is very different than it used to be, thanks to the big patriot Elon Musk), Truth Social brought by President Donald Trump, Telegram (another Truth Fighter), or TikTok brought by CHINA. TikTok should NOT be allowed to operate in the United States, and I hope this is on the President's urgent list. TikTok is one social media platform that I would NEVER use. China is collecting all kinds of information and using it, HOW? I can only imagine. They all started out with great intentions (except CHINA; they started with bad intentions and just got worse), but we know now how it turned out. They all have a tremendous influence, both positive and negative, mostly negative on our society and mostly on our young kids. I can never understand why any parent would let their kids get on these crazy sites. It should be illegal for anyone under the age of 18 to be allowed on any of these social media platforms. Some of these sites are just horrible, some more than others. A good example of a social media platform is "X" under the leadership of Elon Musk. He tries his hardest to make sure no bad actors get on it and spread lies and deception. Truth Social is also a good one, one of the best. Telegram, is also one of the best. Most others are totally to the left and spreading lies and deceit among other things.

All of them must be responsible for what goes on their sites. But there are a lot of problems with them. There are huge concerns about privacy issues, the spread of misinformation, cyberbullying, and many others.

If they are NOT able to control what goes on on their own platform, then the government will have to step in and make some rules. Self-governing just does not work, especially when it comes to sites like Facebook, TikTok, Instagram, or other sites like them. Also, assign a commission to monitor their sites to make sure everything is legal and FAIR.

Food for thought: George Orwell said, *"The most effective way to destroy people is to deny and obliterate their own understanding of their history." Don't allow them to change our history; bring the truth back.*

Hollywood

The Hollywood movie industry is probably the largest movie industry in the world. Their influence is immense all over the world. Unfortunately, this industry is packed with people who have very radical views of what is good for America's foreseeable future. This is totally opposite to most of our country's people's beliefs. Their influence is huge on our kids and our young generation. We are a free country, and I believe that Hollywood has the right to make any movies they want. My problem is when Hollywood is making movies that are supposed to be just entertaining, and they are NOT. So when I spend a good amount of money, drive to the theatre, and when I am in the theatre, I stop and spend more money on candies, a drink, and others, and when I finally sit down to be entertained, halfway through the movie, I am forced to watch a political message incorporated in the movie. That aggravates me very much. I think they are abusing their freedom of speech by stepping all over mine. Any movie that has a political agenda, even the slightest innuendo, should be rated Political/Action. We don't like movies that have messages hidden in them that brainwash us, our younger generation, and even young adults. We all know that they are very impressionable.

And by the way, if the far-left extremists put out lies knowingly and intentionally (and they do know because they have all kinds of checkpoints), they should be charged. For every lie they put out there, they should be charged $1,000,000.00 per episode. Make them stop this way. There is no better way to do it. Hit them where it hurts: THE POCKETBOOK. If they want to play it like that—pay the money. Or better, TELL THE TRUTH. They are going to be broke very soon.

FCC

• So, if I understand this right, the Federal Communications Commission's job is to regulate all communications by radio, wire, television, cable, satellite, or any other type of communication in the United States territories and internationally. But do they really regulate? When they say REGULATE, I thought that they regulate everything, including the content of their speeches, news, or investigative reporting—whatever they put out on the air for everybody to listen to and see on their station. But the FCC, they just don't. They regulate everything BUT that. To me, that is insane. What if one day one of their people goes crazy and decides to go on air and declare that we have been attacked by a nuclear bomb? Can you imagine the mayhem that would follow such a statement? The media on all these types of communication has been, for years, lying to us like crazy, spreading misinformation and propaganda, and much worse things than that. THIS HAS TO STOP FROM HAPPENING. Like carrying the torch for the Democrats. Look at all the lies and misinformation they put out there since Mr. Donald Trump announced his candidacy in 2015.

• Something must be done about this, and very soon. We simply can NOT allow or afford these TV networks to lie with impunity, to go on with business as usual. WE CAN NOT. Their lies on public media change the way people VOTE, which by itself is called ELECTION INTERFERENCE, WHICH IS A CRIME. They change the way we see our everyday life. Some are downright brainwashing. They MUST report the NEWS, NOT MAKE the news. Enough is enough. We all have the right to freedom of speech but NOT the freedom to lie and deceive. You can NOT go into a theater and scream FIRE. We all know that. Well, lying to the masses on TV, radio, social media, etc., is the same as screaming FIRE in the theater. IT HAS GOT TO STOP. There should be huge penalties for every time you break the law on air or whatever public media means of communication might be. This should also go for lying politicians or any public figure that people take as truth-tellers. This is the reason our country has fallen to this low level of TRUST in our government, TV news, and social media. Even when this problem is fixed, it is going to take a long time before the people of this country will regain their TRUST in the politicians, news media, newspapers, and so on.

In light of what has been happening lately in our beautiful nation (President Donald Trump), we better remember what Mr. Martin Luther King said: **"Injustice anywhere is a threat to justice everywhere."**

On Freedom of Speech

• Yes, freedom of speech is great, but it is NOT freedom to LIE. Congress needs and MUST pass a Truth Law. This has to apply to all forms of media: TV, radio, cable TV, newspapers, books, documentaries, social media of any kind, and even the politicians themselves. And yes, EVERY single person that speaks in public. No people in public venues should be allowed to spread lies misinformation, or propaganda whatsoever. Everything has to be backed up by proverbial facts. You can do this in a public square, in the streets where people have a choice to listen to your message or just keep on walking. If caught in a lie, even the smallest of lies, they need and MUST be held responsible and accountable and must be fined (huge fines) and/or have their licenses to operate revoked if they keep this kind of behavior up. This is America, not some Banana Republic. We are the leaders of the world, so we must set an example, and only then can we make a difference and an example that others will follow.

• Everybody and anybody must have the right to speak their mind, but in the proper setting and as long as it does not infringe on anybody else's freedoms. NO one should be allowed to REWRITE USA HISTORY, NO ONE.

• Ronald Reagan said, ***"Status Quo, You Know, Is Latin For, The Mess We Are In."***

AGRICULTURE/FOOD

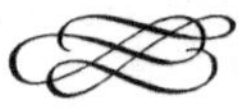

"A Form Of Protectionism Should Be Enforced At The National Level, At Least In Strategic Areas Such As Agriculture." Marion Marechal-Le Pen, Member of the European Parliament. A very wise woman.

• If the government is to do anything for us, is that it should be to safeguard us from the big corporations and, even worse, CHINA. Especially the Chinese. They (China) are buying agricultural lands near American military bases or missile silos. Why is that? Big Corporations are purchasing agricultural land from family businesses and converting it into industrial complexes that use chemicals like never before, chemicals that are slowly killing us all. This is not good for anybody. We and our children are becoming sicker each year. The government must step in and get the facts before it's too late for all of us.

• I believe there must be a law that only organic food can be grown in the USA. It should also be made illegal to produce poisonous synthetic fertilizers and insecticides, which are so destructive to our health and to the environment. And let's not forget all the creatures of the land. We, the people, should demand this. It might be a little more expensive, but it's a lot tastier and far richer in vitamins and minerals essential to our health. We would eat less and be much healthier. Therefore, in the long run, I guarantee it will be cheaper, and you and your family will have a healthier and happier life, and enjoy a happy life, all the time. Think of the alternative. Would you rather pay a little more at the grocery store now for a healthier life, or spend all your life savings and possibly even your family home later on, when you discover you have cancer, a heart attack, diabetes, or who knows what? Consider the pain and grief for your family and yourself. The drugs, often not covered by insurance, will eat into your Social Security. Talk to people who have gone through these situations. People throughout America are getting sicker and sicker; even children are developing diabetes, cancer, and many other diseases at increasingly younger ages.

• Our meat industry is also very corrupt. Whether it's beef, pork, poultry, or fish, it's all full of steroids, hormones, antibiotics, and who knows what else. These are so destructive to our health, and no one is doing anything about it. Many of us are becoming obese and sick. The poorer people are, the more obese they get. Why? Because poor people cannot afford to eat organic foods like meats, vegetables, or fruits. Instead, they consume fast food or junk food from places like KFC, McDonald's, and Burger King because it's more affordable but full of poisons and ultra-processed ingredients. Processed foods have no nutritional value for the human body. Why are we allowing these companies to do this to us?

• THIS MUST STOP. We need to put pressure on our corrupt politicians to take action. We must demand that they enact laws requiring only organic foods to be grown or imported into the United States. The fat cats selling us junk food that makes us sick and obese should be put on notice: change your food, or we change you. Recall and revolt by vote. Politicians, you are now on notice by the American people!

• Look at our healthcare costs. They are the highest in the world, and we have the sickest population per capita of all civilized countries. Why is no one paying attention to this impending catastrophe? Everyone is asleep while something far more sinister is happening. Food corporations are getting away with murder literally. Our food is heavily processed; it must be investigated and stopped. Where is the news media to investigate? We must return to the basics and revert to the way we used to grow plants, fruit trees, and other agricultural products that are so needed. Right now, they are poisoning Americans with ultra-processed foods and chemicals.

• The food-making industries are adding all kinds of drugs, chemicals, synthetic fertilizers, synthetic insecticides, antibiotics, steroids, and other unknown substances to our foods to make them last longer and increase profits. They over-process our food. No drugs or chemicals should be allowed in our food. Sugar, corn syrup, and many other synthetic sweeteners should be banned from all products. They are killing our children, us, and our elders by the hundreds of thousands every year. Do they care about us? NO, THEY DO NOT. We all suffer from various diseases. Our children are suffering from obesity and diabetes at an alarmingly young age.

• "In 2022, Americans paid over $4.5 trillion for healthcare —an astronomical amount of money. Did you know that? I bet not. That's over $13,000 per person, not per family, per person. I didn't know that until I started digging a bit. Do you know how much good could be done for your family with this kind of money? We need to wake up and pressure politicians to change the law and do it fast. ONLY ORGANIC."

• All junk food and drinks must be removed immediately from all schools, by law. Junk food producers must label their products with warnings that they will make consumers sick with cancer, obesity, and heart attacks, and eventually kill them, just like cigarettes. Because this is just as bad as cigarettes if not worse.

• We must turn this country around, and fast. I am with MAGA. Are you?

• *"Agriculture Can Trigger Job-Led Economic Growth, Provided It Becomes Intellectually Satisfying And Economically Rewarding."* M.S. Swaminathan, Father of the Green Revolution in India.

ELECTION

This initiative aims to bring more qualified American patriots into the race for President of the United States, with the goal of leading the nation to a better state than the one we inherited. A President will serve for four years, with the possibility of an additional term if they perform exceptionally well. Currently, the system is too CORRUPT to fix. Influenced by wealthy individuals who control the outcomes behind the scenes. Their puppets follow orders, making the system rigged and in need of comprehensive reform. It must be fair to all future candidates from diverse backgrounds, ensuring everyone has an equal chance to compete.

Here's how I envision fairness in the process. This blueprint is a starting point, though it can be adjusted as

needed. Money must not play any role in electing the right candidate. Importantly, once elected, the candidate should not be influenced by donors, as there will be none. This ensures that the candidate with the best platform for the future of the USA will prevail. This type of election system should apply to all political positions.

• Every person wishing to run for President or any other political position must undergo a rigorous investigation by the NSA, FBI, CIA, State Department, and Interpol. A clean criminal record is mandatory, and candidates should be leaders in their communities with no past scandals. We also have to know DO THEY LOVE AMERICA and THE AMERICAN CONSTITUTION?

• Candidates must possess strong skills in business management or corporate leadership, political experience, and excellent people skills. They should also have some familiarity with leaders of other countries, given that this is one of the most demanding and dangerous jobs in the world.

• To avoid repeating the issues of 2020, candidates must undergo thorough physical and mental medical exams. The country cannot afford a repeat of the situation under Joe Biden, which had global repercussions and resulted in many indirect deaths. The United States is perceived as weak because of these events.

• Once candidates meet initial requirements, they must provide a written statement detailing their platform, political affiliation, and their positions. It is crucial to ascertain there are commitments to America.

• The campaign structure must be redesigned to ensure clarity and fairness.

• First and foremost, candidates should not receive any more money, not even from their own pockets. They will not require funding.

Candidates will be prohibited from speaking about their rivals. Any such action will result in disqualification. This task is handled by the NSA, FBI, DOJ, or INTERPOL during the vetting process. Candidates are allowed only to answer questions during debates, with an opportunity for an opening and closing statement.

1. There will be three debates at each level.

2. The campaign will start at the local level via public broadcasting TV, radio, and potentially social media. Debates will be advertised to reach the largest audience during prime time.

3. All candidates will have the same amount of time for their opening statements.

4. All candidates will be asked the same questions.

5. All candidates will have the same amount of time to answer each question, with no do-overs.

6. All candidates will have the same amount of time for closing statements.

7. Voters will cast their choice via text. After the three debates, the candidate with the most votes will advance to the next level.

Next, candidates will debate at the state level.

The top ten candidates will debate nationally on TV, radio, and social media. The two best candidates—one Republican and one Democrat—will then debate each other in three debates, whether for the House of Representatives, Senate, or Presidency.

The same rules will apply at all stages of the debates.

At each stage, no candidate is allowed to receive any money, under penalty of disqualification or prosecution. With this new system, candidates will not need financial contributions. This approach ensures that the best candidate is elected fairly and squarely. Before starting their campaign, candidates must be endorsed by their political party and provide a signed statement of their intentions and platform in alignment with their party. If elected, they must fully adhere to their promises to the American people.

"Politicians all too often think about the next election. Statesmen think about the next generation." Linda Lingle, former Governor of Hawaii

EDUCATION

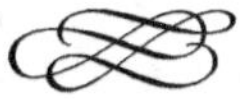

- *"Education is not preparation for life; education is life itself."* John Dewey, an education reformer and philosopher

- President Donald Trump should demand (not ask) that the establishment politicians (both houses of Congress) pass a bill to create charter schools, so all the kids in America will have a fair chance at a great education, equal to anywhere in the country. Every family should be given a voucher to send their kids to any school of their choosing, even if it is a private school (if it is a private school, the parents will have to pay the difference in cost). This is the only way out of gangs and poverty. Give them a GREAT education. Our greatest treasure is our kids. When are the incompetent politicians going to learn this? These politicians will NEVER learn. They MUST be replaced with younger, pro-American, pro-MAGA leaders. The more education, the bigger the treasure. The bigger the treasure, the better for the families. The better the families, the better for America. So TEACH, and TEACH again. Never stop.

• More and more American kids are going to college and other higher learning institutions than ever before. But even as students attend college at record-breaking rates, the country continues to fall behind other nations. For many years, institutions in the United States dominated rankings of the best colleges in the world. Of the top 10 best universities in the world, eight are located in the U.S. But despite having some of the best educational institutions on earth, the Organisation for Economic Co-operation and Development (OECD) ranks the U.S. sixth for adult education levels. Not very good news when you consider the money we spend every year on education. We MUST educate our kids to learn how to think, how to process information, and how to adapt. Our country has some of the best natural resources, from gold to oil to just about anything you can think of. But it is not enough. We must take good care of our kids and give them the best education money can buy. They ARE the real TREASURE.

• Malcolm X said many times: ***"Education is the passport to the future, for tomorrow belongs to those who prepare for it today." Keep that in mind our dear politicians.***

• On that note, I think our government is making a huge mistake by allowing kids of our enemy, CHINA, to come to the U.S. and get the best education in our schools and research centers while taking the places and opportunities of our American kids to excel. Many foreigners have been trained in industrial espionage (especially so-called Chinese kids). They get to steal away for free all kinds of research and technologies, such as aviation and AI, worth billions of dollars. The last time I checked, over $500 billion every year is lost due to industrial espionage. No kids from enemy countries should ever be allowed to come to America and study. NONE. End of story.

• For that to happen, we MUST first ensure we have great teachers to educate our kids. While nominal teacher salaries have increased over the last couple of decades, when adjusted for inflation, the average salary has dropped over time—about 1.3% lower than the $61,275 (in 2017-2018). This is wrong. This MUST be fixed also. While many teachers earn a solid middle-class wage, the job comes with unique challenges. Many teachers across the U.S. end up spending a not-insignificant amount of their take-home pay on school supplies for their students and classrooms. That should NEVER happen.

• In the following countries, kids are getting a better education than in the United States: Canada, Japan, Israel, Korea, and the United Kingdom. We are in 6th place. You could say, "not bad." You might be right, but we spend a heck of a lot more money on education than the other countries. Let's learn from them.

• *"The essence of living is giving."* A Wise man said. We should teach this to all our kids from an early age and throughout their lives into adulthood. The world would be a much better place than it is today. I grew up with this principle and lived my life by it. Sometimes I gave to the wrong people and didn't keep enough for myself. Well, I am still happy, and I learned to give a little to myself as well.

• Kids MUST be taught how to dream and dream big. "Dreaming is achieving." I didn't say that; I just heard it when I was a young man, and I never forgot it. I always dream big.

• Benjamin Franklin: *"An investment in knowledge pays the best interest."*

• In order to save our children and the future of humanity, we MUST teach our kids, once a week, a very important and strong health education program. From kindergarten through 12th grade and maybe throughout university.

• We first have to teach the little kids how to start the day:

- Make their bed as soon as they get out of it.
- Wash, at least your hands, face, and teeth.
- Follow a little exercise every morning.

- Eat the right foods to stay healthy. No junk foods or drinks should be allowed in any school, by law. The junk food industries are making our kids sick.
- How to take care of their bodies.
- How to have a healthy lifestyle.
- About the human body.
- Learn what is best for us, what constitutes healthy food, and what is unhealthy. Only then will we have a much healthier society. We will spend much less on healthcare, and people will be more productive and happier.
- No junk foods or drinks should be allowed in any school, by law. The junk food industries are making our kids sick.

• Understanding the truth that **exercising, eating healthily, no stress and resting are all part of it**, and we will all be that much healthier and better off. It's a MUST. We need to do it because society needs us to help wherever we can.

• Political and Spiritual Leader Mahatma Gandhi said; **Live As If You Were To Die Tomorrow. LEARN As If You Were To Live Forever.** " Very good idea, I heard this years ago and I will never stop learning.

POLITICIANS

John Adams, one of our Founding Fathers, said: *"Fear is the foundation of most governments."*

Biden, the DOJ, and the rest of the co-conspirators who came up with the four different indictments on 91 counts, 67 of which are in New York alone, each one more dubious than the last, nothing but smoke and mirrors. They just did interfere with the Presidential election of 2024. That is a crime. It will be proven very soon.

And we would do well to remember what Marcus Aurelius said: *"Everything we hear is an opinion, NOT a fact. Everything we see is a perspective, NOT the truth."* So, don't rush to believe everything you hear and see, get the facts.

The next President, Donald Trump of the United States MUST form a commission of 12 investigators: 3

Republicans, 3 Independents, 3 Democrats, and 3 Libertarians. Start the investigation at the top with Biden and his family first for the true crimes he committed as Vice President and later as President against the United States. Just follow the money. Senators and Congressmen should be next; again, follow the money. Start with the richest politicians and work your way down. How did they make tens and some of them hundreds of millions of dollars on their salary as a politician? Even the judges and prosecutors that were involved should be investigated. They are all part of this conspiracy. Just apply the law and show no mercy.

What about the DOJ or FBI, the State Department, NSA? Just asking. Were they involved in it?

People like Adam Schiff, this despicable Congressman who spent months waving a bunch of papers on TV in our faces, claiming he had concrete evidence against President Donald Trump, was lying through his teeth and knew it then. It was Hillary Clinton who did that, all along. Yet Schiff dared to look us in the eye and lie. For this and so many other times he lied to us with a smirk on his face, he should be thrown out on his keister. He is a professional liar. He was not the only one putting on this circus. Oh no, there were many others, including Hillary Clinton—the chief liar, crook, and criminal, the worst of them all. I don't think I gave her too much credit, do you?

Show the American people and the world that corruption in the United States is unacceptable and will be stopped by applying the full extent of the law. We have to ensure we have very solid evidence.

All politicians or leaders MUST be held responsible for the words that come out of their mouths on TV and in any public place. They are working for the people, not the people for them. Misinformation, as it is today, goes unchecked, so this is very important.

Nobody should serve as a politician for more than two terms, period. Just as the President cannot serve more than two terms, this rule should apply to all politicians.

The reason they hate President Donald Trump so much is that he is telling the truth and undoing everything American haters and communists have been undermining the American way of life, history, and family values.

Warren Buffett said, **"I could end the deficit in 5 minutes,"** **he told CNBC. "You just pass a law that says that anytime there is a deficit of more than 3% of GDP, all sitting members of Congress are ineligible for re-election."** That is a very good idea. The 26th Amendment (granting the right to vote for 18-year-olds) took only 3 months and 8 days to be ratified! Why? Simple! The people demanded it. That was in 1971, before computers, email, cell phones, etc. Of the 27 amendments to the Constitution, seven took 1 year or less to become the law of the land—all because of **public pressure.**

Some of the Congressional Reform Act of 2011, plus some of my ideas. Lots of public pressure MUST be applied.

• No tenure / No pension. A Congressman collects a salary while in office and receives no extra pay or benefits when they are out of office. Period.

• No insider trading anymore. The law is the law. They are not above the law. All laws MUST be applicable 100% to all citizens alike.

• Congress (past, present, and future) MUST participate in Social Security. All funds in the Congressional retirement fund move to the Social Security system immediately. All future funds flow into the Social Security system, and Congress participates like the rest of the American people.

• Social Security funds cannot be used for any other purpose, not even borrowed.

• Congress can purchase their own retirement plan, just as all Americans do.

• Congress will no longer vote themselves a pay raise. Congressional pay will rise by whichever is the lower of CPI or 3%

• Congress loses its current health care system and participates in the same health care system as the American people.

• Congress must equally abide by all laws they impose on the American people. The law is for all Americans the same.

• All contracts with past and present Congressmen are to be void as of January 2026. The American people did not make these contracts with Congressmen; Congressmen made these contracts for themselves. How convenient. Serving in Congress is an honor, not a career. You are a public servant. Don't be confused about that. The Founding Fathers envisioned citizen legislators, not professional legislators. They should serve their term or two and then go home and back to work.

• Lord Acton once wrote to a friend: **"The same moral standards should be applied to all men, Political and Religious Leaders Included, Especially Since Power Tends to Corrupt and Absolute Power Corrupts Absolutely."** We must remember this, and remember it very well.

• Make lobbying illegal. No exceptions. There is too much influence for big corporations and special groups

• Implement two-term limits for any Senator and House of Representative: Two 4-year terms. That's plenty of time to make a difference if you are effective. If not face recall and go home after two years.

• A leader of the country should have a family—wife and children—or else they have no personal stake in the fight for America.

• Misinformation should be severely punished by law. This is very important.

• No smearing of anyone in any way, shape, or form in public should be allowed. Make it law. If caught, pay substantial fines and face potential jail time. There is far too much of this happening. If you have evidence of crimes committed, report them to the FBI. Let them handle it. They know how.

• All parties, including Republicans, Democrats, Independents, and Libertarians, should release a statement on their platform: straightforward and to the point. This statement should be published online so that the public can download it. Everyone should be able to read it and hold the respective party accountable in the next election cycle.

• Why doesn't someone monitor all judges, regardless of their party affiliation? They should uphold the law and be assessed for performance and impartiality. Take Alvin Bragg, for example, prosecuting Donald Trump while not allowing him to discuss the trial and having a jury mostly composed of Democrats. This raises concerns about election interference and bias. He should be monitored, and if necessary, prosecuted. It is crucial to ensure that those involved in significant trials uphold the law.

• Pay close attention to what Franklin Roosevelt once said: **"In politics, nothing happens by accident. If it happens, you can bet it was planned that way."**

• A perfect example of this is Barack Hussein Obama. This was no accident; he was strategically positioned by politicians and the far-left media. He transitioned from being a professor to the presidency in just a few short years. Joe Biden referred to Obama as a "clean" African American candidate. What was he implying? Obama was a civil rights attorney who ran for the Illinois Senate, served for 7 years, and then ran for the U.S. Senate and served as a senator. He had little impact during his tenure and was known as one of the most liberal senators. When he won the presidency in 2008, what did he deliver? Affordable Care that MOST Citizens could not afford. Did he profit from it? And why? What did he do for the devastated Black communities across the country? Absolutely nothing. He had 8 years and a significant opportunity to improve those neglected neighborhoods and their children's education, but he did NOTHING.

• This illustrates the problem of appointing someone to lead the country who lacks managerial or people skills, doesn't understand the system, and seems intent on undermining the country. It's time to educate American citizens and university students about the responsibility of choosing a president. It's not necessarily about finding a politician, but a great businessman. Oh, and don't forget a great PATRIOT. The country operates like a vast business, and it requires someone with exceptional managerial and people skills. If the individual is also a politician, all the better. To be the President of the United States is the most powerful position in the free world. All candidates must undergo extensive medical and mental evaluations before they can even begin their campaign.

• Here's a little wisdom from John F. Kennedy: *"If you make peaceful revolution impossible, you make violent revolution inevitable."*

On Incompetence

• Whenever certain people are called to testify before Congress, for whatever reason, they should be fully prepared. If they answer with "I do not know," "I do not recall," or "I'm not in charge of that," they should be fired on the spot. This is unacceptable. Congress should not accept this kind of behavior anymore. They are in charge of certain departments and should answer the questions. They must prepare to provide all the answers—yes or no, nothing more. No stories, excuses, or wasting millions of American dollars to avoid answering questions. They MUST answer.

Progressive Movement

- The progressive movement is nothing but anarchists. Their goal is to create chaos so they can take over the government and rule without any laws or constitutions. Progressives would like you to believe they are socialists or even communists. Far from it, they are much worse. They are not advocates of law and order (if it were up to them, they would defund police departments everywhere). These people are, at best, anarchists. They seek as much chaos as possible to get rich and gain control.

- An example of the progressive movement: In November 1994, during the California General Election, voters passed Proposition 187, also known as the "Save Our State" initiative. The proposition aimed to deny public services, such as education, healthcare, welfare, and other benefits, to anyone in the United States illegally due to the fiscal burden on California's people. However, in 1997, the proposition was struck down as unconstitutional by the Federal District Court and the Ninth Circuit U.S. Court of Appeals. This was the will of the people of California, but the courts, packed with progressive judges, overturned it. As a result, taxes in California increased significantly.

- Progressives want as much chaos as possible. They profit from it and seek more control.

On Socialism

• Show me how many people from the USA try to sneak into Russia, North Korea, or China illegally, and I'll show you millions from all over the world trying to migrate to the USA legally or illegally.

Remember this: Thomas Jefferson said, *"A government afraid of its citizens is a democracy. Citizens afraid of government is tyranny."*

REVOLT BY VOTE

Voting is both a right and a Responsibility for ALL American citizens. It is a powerful tool that allows us to participate in our democratic process and elect individuals who qualify and genuinely want to serve the public. By voting, we can make America a better place for our children, grandchildren, and future generations. However, recent elections have seen a disappointing outcome, with politicians like AOC and her squad, along with others in the House of Representatives and Senate, taking office. These individuals, elected to critical positions, often create laws that make life more difficult, increase taxes, and diminish our liberty. They seem to prioritize their own interests over those of the country, aiming to maintain power rather than foster prosperity. Look at figures like Mitch McConnell, Bernie Sanders, Chuck

Grassley, Angus King, Richard Blumenthal, Nancy Pelosi, Steny Hoyer, Hal Rogers, Bill Pascrell, Grace Napolitano, Maxine Waters, Jim Clyburn, Danny Davis, Frederica Wilson, and many more. It's truly alarming. These politicians, many of whom have been in office for decades, are out of touch with reality and, in some cases, seem to despise America while enjoying its financial benefits. They would rather impose tyranny than uphold democratic principles.

We need to VOTE THEM OUT on November 5, 2024. This year represents a pivotal moment for our country. Let's seize the opportunity to support President Donald Trump and "REVOLT by VOTE." Let's remove these long self-serving politicians and make room for young, passionate Americans ready to fight for our nation. This is America's chance to clean house, to replace ineffective leaders with vibrant, dedicated individuals who love this country. REVOLT by VOTE.

It's time for the new generation to step up and contribute to this beautiful United States of America that we all cherish. However, we need a new system for electing politicians. The current system is broken and impossible to fix. The super-rich and the media dictate the outcomes, manipulating the process and controlling what people see and hear. Politicians lie to Americans, betraying their trust. **See Chapter 7 on Elections.**

We must use our voting power to challenge the "status quo." Vote immediately to remove politicians who failed to deliver on their campaign promises, particularly those who have been in office for over twelve years, Revolt by Vote and throw out AOC and her squad. The stakes are too high to offer second chances. We cannot afford to waste more time. We are on the brink of disaster. This applies to all levels of politics: local, state, and national. We need to clean houses across the country. We must vote to support or oppose any initiative or policy, such as tax increases, that the government considers implementing. With the internet and national ID, we should be able to vote every day if necessary. We MUST exercise our right to "REVOLT, by VOTE" when appropriate.

Let's shape America according to our vision, not the politicians' or the media's. They seek to rule us with an iron fist of TYRANNY. Always verify your facts, preferably from sources like Truth Social, "X," or Telegram, rather than CNN or CNBC. We should hold American haters and TV stations accountable for their lies and propaganda.

Remember: Voting is not only our right but our RESPONSIBILITY.

Voting is the most powerful tool we, as American citizens, have to force (non-violent) change the way "we the people" want them to be.

Participate in this democratic process to create positive changes in our society. REVOLT by VOTE. It's a call to change America the way it was meant to be. **Free. Bring back the American Dream**

Vote every time you get the opportunity. Make a difference. Teach your kids to vote as well; take them with you while they are still too young to vote. It's crucial to our survival as a country. When you're angry about something, REVOLT by VOTE. I believe it should be law that politicians serve only two four-year terms. Furthermore, if they don't perform as promised within two years, we should be able to recall them. Why waste another two years on ineffective leaders? They have a country to run—so let them run it. As they say, "Shit or get off the pot." Time for wasting is over. - IT'S TIME FOR ACTION NOW!

The famous football coach Vince Lombardi used to say, *"The greatest accomplishment is not in never falling, but in rising again after you fall."* Let America rise like the Phoenix.

The United States of America, thanks to our crooked and incompetent politicians, has been declining for many years. Let's rise up and show the world our American GRIT and RESILIENCE. Throughout our history, we have been known for these two great qualities. America consistently demonstrates its ability to overcome adversity and emerge stronger than before. Americans are known for our "can do" attitude and willingness to take risks. This is why America leads in technology and scientific achievements. We just don't give up.

LET'S DO IT ONE MORE TIME. GOD BLESS AMERICA

The United States of America will rise like the PHOENIX

I urge all Americans, regardless of political affiliation—Republican, Democrat, Independent, Libertarian, or otherwise; Asian, Latino, White, African American, etc.—to support Donald Trump and vote on November 5, 2024. If we don't vote, America as we know it will be lost forever. It could become a tyranny, a police state, or even a dictatorship. What has been done to Mr. Donald Trump and others from his group, are absolutely CRIMINAL. Just imagine what they could do to you and me. It's unimaginable that this is happening here in the United States of America. We have become a banana republic. Thank you, President Biden and President Obama, you got the ball rolling.

All those involved—from judges to prosecutors are committing a crime by interfering with the election, and they must be held accountable wherever the law was broken.

Everyone in the country should have the chance to compete for the presidency, not just billionaires. There are many capable individuals in business, like Donald Trump and Vivek Ramaswamy, among others. People should compete in ways that do not require vast amounts of money. Public TV stations should be available for debates, starting at the county level, then the state level, and finally at the federal level. **See Chapter 7 on Elections for complete details.**

On Indifference

Some time ago, Obama said that indifference is the biggest threat to our democracy. For once, and probably the only time in my life, I couldn't agree with him more.

It was indifference that allowed a man with no experience in leadership, let alone the experience needed to lead the free world, to gain power. It was indifference that allowed him and his gang of Communists to shamelessly remain President of this beautiful USA for four more years and attempt to destroy our way of life with their Marxist policies.

But guess what? People woke up. No more indifference. Hence, President Donald Trump. America is going to be great again. Because people are indifferent **anymore.**

Here Comes the New Dawn of the United States of America. Get ready for the greatest time in American history. Renascence 2.0, MAGA and President Donald Trump

TRADE / ECONOMY

Phil Knight said, *"I do believe that international trade agreements MUST benefit both nations, ALWAYS."*

That is a great saying; unfortunately, our incompetent politicians don't see it that way.

China is out to destroy every country's economy as the United States, Canada, and every other country in Europe, and our politicians will just let them. If they haven't done it already, then all these countries will be at their mercy. What insanity. Am I the only one seeing this? Really? This has been going on for at least 30 years. We didn't just help them economically but, more importantly, militarily. By now, they could probably crush the Russian army any time they wanted. Poor Russia; they just made a pact with the Chinese to help each other in case of an attack by NATO or the USA.

It's like a mouse, Russia, making a pact with a cat, China. It's just laughable. I didn't realize President Vladimir Putin was that gullible. And where did he get the idea that NATO or the USA would ever attack them? And WHY?

We MUST right this ship. A new trade policy MUST be created and enforced, with each country (the European Union considered as one country) in mind. Trade with any country must be fair and balanced. By fair, I mean that the prices of products brought into the USA MUST be comparable in quality and price to products made in America. If prices are too low, the US government should impose an extra tax to level the playing field. By balance, I mean that we MUST export to the trading country as much as we import from them. For years, China has gotten away with exporting $750 billion more to the USA each year than it imports from us. What is wrong with this picture? I'll tell you what: it means that for years, the American treasury loses $750 billion to China every year—a fortune. Imagine over the last 20 years; that adds up to over $15 trillion dollars. On top of that, add approximately $500 billion per year in stolen intellectual property through industrial espionage. Over 20-25 years, that totals another $10 trillion. Total loss to the US Treasury: $25 trillion.

What is the American debt today? I think about $34 trillion. Take away the $25 trillion lost to China, and we are down to $9 trillion. Now remove the immense interest we have had to pay on that $34 trillion over the years, and we are down to virtually nothing. THANK YOU, CHINA. And thank you, American politicians. You did an outstanding job. For yourselves.

John Barrasso said, ***"When it comes to international trade, the question is, who is going to write the rules, the United States or China? And my vote is THE UNITED STATES."***

So let's get it done. Mr. President Trump, write new rules. We've been screwed long enough. Let's fix it.

Personally, I think trade is a fantastic and powerful tool that the USA could and should use with all the countries of the world that are friendly to us. NO TRADE with our enemies. NONE whatsoever. Screw them, let them trade with each other. Don't be fooled by our politicians; CHINA is our biggest ENEMY. They think they can take us. Let's open the doors of diplomacy to all countries that are on the fence because of our past history with them. But if anyone can pull this off quickly, it's President Donald Trump. We should also look at the African continent. It holds immense potential. Huge market. China has been there for years, swindling every country they made deals with. The leaders of these countries have a very sour taste in their mouths from dealing with China and some don't know how to escape these deals. Let's help them out and see what happens. Let's teach them how to work the land, bring their brightest medical students here, and provide the equipment they need. They need help in so many fields. It's a huge opportunity for the United States. It's a vast continent with a huge market. Somalia, Yemen, and many other poor countries would all benefit from this. We must offer them, above all else, a great educational system. Build schools for them and educate them on how to teach the kids. That way, they will have a bright future for themselves, their kids, and the entire African continent. It's a WIN-WIN situation.

I must insist: Let's bring manufacturing back to America. Let's make the brand "MADE IN AMERICA" famous again. Let's make American workers proud of what they are doing. Let's show the world that the USA WILL BE REBORN AND RISE AGAIN.

On the Super-Rich Companies

• How about corporations that make billions and billions of dollars in profit year after year? I would love to see them think a little more about their employees, paying them more money that would improve their quality of life. These companies would end up with much more loyal workers. In turn, this would also benefit the American economy and show the world American generosity.

• ***Be generous, and you will have a much richer life.***

HEALTH INSURANCE

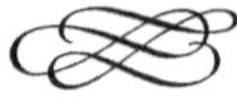

Quote by Tom Harkin; " America's Healthcare System Is In Crisis Precisely Because We Systematically Neglect Wellness And Prevention."

• Before I dive into the Health Insurance issue, I want to comment on the pandemic situation. It should have NEVER happened. It only happened because our incompetent politicians and Dr. Fauci wanted it to. They planned it that way all along. They shut down the country for so long that most small businesses went under. Who benefited from this crazy and insane decision? BIG BUSINESS, CHINA, Fauci, and certain politicians. They made a fortune. China is the one giving a ton of money to our politicians every year. Screw the small businesses who need them? And all the millions of workers that were out of their jobs? Who cares about them? Oh Yes, they got some money for a while from the government, just to get by. and now?

• If they really wanted to stop the pandemic, all they had to do was pass a law that if you were caught in public with any transmittable disease, including Covid-19, you would pay a huge fine and go to jail, just to drive the point really well. Do you think we would have had a Pandemic situation? NO. You wouldn't have had a pandemic situation whatsoever. NONE. The Chinese benefited the most from this situation. That was our thanks to them for bringing Covid-19 to us and to the world. Thank you, Dr. Fauci. After 36 years in business, I lost everything due to the decisions Dr. Fauci made for us. I wonder how much money Dr. Fauci made from the Covid-19 situation. I know the country lost trillions of dollars while China made trillions. Bravo to Dr. Fauci, you were a genius.

• Big Pharma and the food industry are killing Americans or making them and their children very sick by the millions every year with their drugs and overprocessed foods (junk foods).

• Pre-teens, teens, and young adults are getting diabetes, cancer, and other diseases at a very young age. Like never before. Grown-ups are no exception. We would not have these diseases if our food weren't so full of steroids, antibiotics, pesticides, and who knows what else. This is just regarding meat, but all our produce is also full of harmful chemicals. We are getting sicker than ever before. Our quality of life is far from what it used to be just 50 years ago. Who is going to stop these corporations from harming the American people? Almost everyone I know suffers from some disease. This should NEVER happen. We all suffer so much while the food industries get filthy rich. This is all due to the type of food they are selling us, the American people. When you go to any supermarket today, you will find that over 90% of the food they sell is processed and over-processed food. This means these foods have NO nutritional value for us. And when the body does not get what it needs we get the urge to eat more and more of the same crap food and HENCE overweight kids and people. When foods have shelf lives for months and even years, in some cases, you know it can't be good for you, let alone for your kids. We deserve much better than this.

• When it comes to Big Pharma, they are just as guilty as the food industries. They spend billions of dollars every year to brainwash future doctors into using more and more drugs. They even offer bonuses per prescription. But they don't spend a dime to have universities teach future doctors how to prevent these diseases. All these diseases ARE PREVENTABLE. It's all about lifestyle, food, sleep, and exercise. But of course, they wouldn't do that. Come on, they are not stupid. CRIMINALS YES, stupid, NO. They know exactly what they are doing. They would lose billions in drug sales if they did that. They MUST be made to do it. There is no limit to their GREED. So who is going to fix this problem? Politicians? NO, not a chance, not the ones in power now, I guarantee it. We, the people, MUST apply pressure on them and make them change or "Revolt, by Vote." Throw those bums out, vote them out, and elect a new, younger generation of politicians who have young kids at home and are willing to fight for us as for themselves. They understand our pain. Our quality of life is declining rapidly.

• If we care about our country, we should put pressure on politicians to pass laws for organic food in the USA. Processed food should come with a large warning label, just like cigarettes. This food will eventually KILL you. Processed foods are much worse than cigarettes because we feed our kids and ourselves without knowing how harmful they are.

• For now, we need to do our part and teach young parents how to feed their children properly and how to exercise with them. All schools MUST remove junk food and sugary drinks from their grounds and replace them with fresh fruits and vegetables. Teachers MUST educate children about which foods are beneficial and which are harmful. Every school day should start with some stretching and mild exercise. Kids will perform much better as a result.

• Doctors should be able to advise their patients on proper diet and exercise. They should learn this in Universities. Today's doctors should be made to take courses about nutrition and Preventive Medicine. They should help their patients change their lifestyles if they want to live long, healthy, and happy lives. Doctors need to spend more time with each patient if they truly care, no more quick 10-minute visits followed by "I'll see you next time." Teach patients not to drink and why not to drink, smoke, or consume processed foods. This includes anything in a jar, bag, box, or other packaging. Gradually, people will start eating healthier, taking their knowledge home, and feeding their families the same way, leading to a healthier and happier society.

• The way I see it, both Democrats and Republicans MUST work together, for America's sake and their own family's sake, and pass laws holding the food industry and Big Pharma criminally responsible for deaths due to bad food and excessive drug use. This is the health CRISIS Americans are facing today. And it is getting worse every day, every minute even as I am writing these words now. Sick, obese, depressed, and suicidal, this is what most of us are facing every day. It's a shame. How did we get here, and more importantly, how do we get out of this horrible situation? Our politicians have sold their souls to Big Pharma and the Food Industry. We need people who will fight for us, the American Citizens. We MUST vote out all politicians who have been in office for over 12 years. We need a younger generation, those with young children of their own, who understand the situation better. A healthy America will be a happy and more productive America. Let's start over on November 5th, 2024.

Mental Institutions

• We should reinstate asylum hospices for people who are mentally unstable. These individuals currently have no proper place to go for care. They are often released to their families, and then only God knows what happens. But they always end up in the streets, where they pose a danger to themselves and the public. We MUST reestablish long-term care institutions for these individuals. We can't allow them to be homeless. At one point in their lives, they were productive citizens who paid taxes. It is not right to treat them like stray animals.

Health Care Insurance

• I want to address health insurance premiums because they are utterly unfair and crazy expensive. This issue MUST be resolved by Republicans once and for all, and quickly. For God's sake, stop postponing this problem. Why do you make it so difficult? It is NOT as difficult as you might think. Relly. Look, just use the car insurance model. Do all car owners pay their premiums based on their age? NO.

• Car owners and drivers must complete a huge questionnaire with many variables. Apply the same model to health insurance but adapt it to individual habits. Questions could include: How old are you? Are you a vegetarian? Do you smoke or have you ever smoked? Do you use or have you ever used drugs? What kind of medication do you take? How tall are you? How much do you weigh? Do you exercise? If so, how much and what kind? How much and what type of alcohol do you consume? Do you have any existing conditions? ….. Let the insurance companies figure it out, don't worry. They know this better than you guys.

• Before insuring someone, conduct a thorough physical examination to confirm the accuracy of the questionnaire. Reward those with good health and habits by lowering their premiums and increasing the payments for those who are not so health-conscious. This will provide a strong incentive for people to improve their health year after year.

• Every year, conduct another thorough physical examination and adjust premiums accordingly. It's not that complicated, is it? NO IS NOT.

• You don't see people driving without car insurance, do you? So make sure people have health insurance as well. Use a carrot-and-stick approach. Why should you and I pay for others' lack of insurance or bad behavior? NO WAY. No Insurance pays CASH, That is all. He/she will get it next time. Or even better make everyone have proof of insurance.

• Defense Secretary Jim Mattis on Tuesday called it a "sad state of affairs" when most of America's young males cannot qualify for military service due to obesity or drug use. "It's a sad state of affairs when 71 percent of 18 to 24-year-old males in this country cannot qualify to enter the United States Army as a private," he told cadets at the Virginia Military Institute. Wow, that is totally unacceptable.

• The solution to saving and resolving the healthcare problem is to educate people and doctors to change their approach. From kindergarten through high school and into universities students MUST have at least one hour per week dedicated to nutrition and health education. If this happens, there won't be any obese people, general sickness will decrease, and the healthcare crisis will be addressed.

• Forget about comprehensive health insurance—it will NEVER happen. Focus on ONE thing at a time. Soon, you'll achieve everything and win election after election. Do what people want and need NOW.

• Billions of dollars are lost every year due to insurance fraud, and doctors are often involved in these scams. What a shame! People like this should go to prison for a minimum of 20 years. The price is just too high if they are caught. They and others will never do it again. There needs to be a system of checks and balances in this industry. We are all paying extra to cover for these criminals or for people without health insurance. Ensure that everyone pays into the system.

• Somebody said: *"Health insurance is not a luxury; it's a necessity. It's not a want, it's a need. And it's a matter of life and death."*

FAMILY UNIT

"It's Not What We Have in Life, But Who We Have in Our Life That Matters." By Jean M. Laurence, A Canadian Novelist. This is so true. wise man.

• We need to go back 50-60 years and look at family life then to see what it was like in the 60s and 70s. Wow, what a difference. To begin with, family unity was very, very strong. On Sundays, almost all families spent time together with their kids, either at home or at church, or both. There was only one TV per family, not one for each member of the family. They would have breakfast in the morning and then go to church together. Americans loved the Lord, and most of us still do. After that, it was more family time. We would meet other family members and get together for a barbecue at one of their houses or just go out for lunch together. Later, we would play some games in the backyard. When this activity was over, sometimes we would take a short nap and later have a small dinner, mostly leftovers. Finally, the family close to the evening would gather around the TV, one per household, to watch a movie or a show together and talk about it afterward. The movies and the family shows then, were such that everybody could watch, young and old, without worrying about inappropriate content. And that was a typical Sunday.

During the rest of the week, kids went to school. The quality of education then was a hundred times better than today's schools. Teachers were respected by both kids and parents, and they actually taught the required curriculum. Kids would go home, finish their schoolwork, and then go out to play. Before going to sleep, they would read something or watch TV for half an hour. Then, there were no Smartphones, ha, ha, ha. Adults went to work (approximately 50% of women worked as well). Homemakers would often help with the kids of their working neighbors. At dinner time, there was a lot of conversation about all kinds of subjects, mostly school-related, sports, and yes even politics. There was a lot of love among us. To kids today, this type of activity might seem "lame," but they just don't know what they're missing.

• Today, most kids grow up by themselves. Most times both parents work long hours, and by the time they come home, they are exhausted. By that time, the kids are already home, watching TV or, worse, playing games on their smartphones or texting on social media. Forget about homework, grades don't matter anymore. Talking to each other is a rarity. Parents are too tired of it, and kids are taught in school that we are out of touch with everything. We just don't know anything, they are told. You kids go home and teach your parents what is going on. How do you like that?

• Life was very simple then, and I can hardly remember anyone saying, "I am so stressed out" or "I am so bored." Life was also much more affordable. You could buy a brand-new car with six months' salary. In the early 1970s, the price of gas was (sit down, please) $0.36 per gallon. Today, it can be up to $7.00 per gallon. Thank you, President Biden. You are awesome. We have too much money and don't know what to do with it. Thank you. Oh, and the price of food was also very cheap. What you buy for $100 today would have cost around less than $10.00. The food was also of 100% better quality than today's food.

• I mentioned that I bought my first house in the mid, 1970s. The price for the house was equivalent to my salary for two years, then. Taxes were much lower as well, and rents were considerably cheaper. What can I say? I miss those days a lot. I could go on forever, but I think I've made my point.

• **LIFE WAS VERY GOOD THEN.**

• What a difference today; it really feels like a different world. Life is so much harder, more complicated, and full of stress. There are 6 and 7-year-old kids who will tell you they have so much stress. Are you kidding me? From what? Too good of a living? I don't even know where to start, honestly.

• Many people today have kids out of wedlock, and if that isn't bad enough, the fathers don't even want to get involved financially or personally with their kids. What a shame, that kids grow up on the streets without a father's guidance, in areas full of gangs, drug sales, and dangers at every corner. I would be scared for my own life walking some of our streets. Kids go to schools where they are not taught the curriculum but instead are brainwashed about political, and social issues, homosexuality, bisexuality, communism, and who knows what else. It should be illegal. Teachers are paid to teach a specific curriculum, not to brainwash our kids. This kind of teacher should be held responsible for not teaching what they are paid to teach or be fired. You just can't trust the public educational system today. Kids graduating from most public high schools don't have the reading skills of a seventh-grader. Forget about Math or Science. Are you serious? How are they going to survive in college? They are not. This is exactly what the elites want—too many educated people pose too much competition and a threat. Smart, educated kids would soon figure out the system and become Conservatives/Republicans.

• The value of the dollar has become so weak that even a couple making very good money would have a hard time coming up with a down payment for a house, let alone making the monthly payments afterward. If parents help them out, they still can't manage the monthly payments. It's a horrible situation for young couples just starting out and wanting to have kids. On the other hand, rents are sky-high and unaffordable. So what do you do? They either live in poverty or with their parents if they can. Some move far from work, where houses are somewhat cheaper, driving an hour or more each way, leaving no time for family once they get home. They are just too tired. It's a shame that this is what America has become today. "It's a dog-eat-dog world out there." Something MUST be done about this. American Patriots let every one of us go out and vote. VOTE for a better America, VOTE for a better life for your kids and grandkids, and VOTE for President Donald Trump an American Patriot.

• Many young people today don't even want to work anymore. They receive free money from the government, a situation exacerbated by the pandemic. People get just enough money to get by and have become accustomed to that, so why work? No healthy person, man or woman, should be given a red cent for nothing. Yes, get a job. That is called life. Get off your ass and find something to do. Look for an opportunity, NOT just a big salary. Work your way up from there. Be smart, not like the rest of your peers. Be assertive and proud no matter what you are doing. You are working, not stealing or begging. Hard work always pays off.

Possible Government Solution:

• The government should develop a system of incentives and encourage young people to get married, have kids, and stay married.

• To get married, provide them with a down payment for an apartment. It's a great start.

• To have children, offer them an allowance and tax credits every year for the first two kids until they turn 18 years old.

• For a third child, there should be no taxes until the youngest turns 18 years old.

• Implement higher taxes for adults who are not married.

• Implement higher taxes for married couples who do not have any children.

This approach will pay off significantly down the road. It would be beneficial to America's future and happier families. A safer America.

The happiest people don't have the best of everything; they just make the best of everything they have. So true. I am one of these crazy, happy people. Thank you mom and thank you God for this quality.

HOMELESSNESS AMERICA

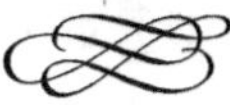

- This is a significant issue in the USA and must be addressed. We should all be ashamed of the current situation in this beautiful country. We have lost many of our beautiful cities to homelessness. Crime rates in these areas are much higher than in most other areas. The places where they sleep are filthy, with trash everywhere, drugs, syringes with exposed needles, and people being threatened for money. Real estate values are declining, employers are losing employees, companies are moving out of state, and tourists are avoiding these cities altogether. The Citizens moving out of state. The economic cost is in the billions annually. We must address this issue by evaluating each individual to understand why they are homeless. Many have serious mental health issues and pose a danger to themselves and their communities. Depending on their mental health status, they should be placed in institutions where they can receive care until doctors deem them safe to return to their families. Families must take responsibility for their well-being. They should **NOT** be released back into the streets. NEVER. Families MUST be responsible for their own and if not, they MUST let the proper Authority know the situation..

• Others may be drug addicts, which is also a widespread issue in this country. These individuals are a danger to themselves and the public at large. They must be taken to hospitals for detoxification programs and kept there until deemed safe to return to their families or friends. The family or friends must take responsibility for their well-being at all times. Again, they should **not** be released into the streets. If any problem again let the proper authority know the situation.

• Some are runaway children of all ages. They should be interviewed to address their issues with their families. If that approach fails, they must be enrolled in a work program and wear an electronic bracelet to ensure they adhere to the program.

• Many are in the country illegally. They must be arrested and deported immediately to their countries of origin. All benefits should be stopped immediately for these individuals. This includes phones, money, health care, debit cards, and other benefits. They must be deported immediately.

• Way too many of these homeless people are American heroes. The American Veterans, this is a slap in our collective faces. How can we ask our kids to go to war in foreign lands and when they come home injured we let them rot in our streets? This is so wrong on so many levels we should all be ashamed of this. These Human beings who put their life on the line should be taken care of like only Heroes deserve. Nothing but the best. They should be medically taken care of, they should be retrained to do something productive, and they should have a place to call home. NOT sleeping in the filthy streets.

A new federal law should be enacted that makes homelessness illegal everywhere in the country. No exceptions.

The economy will improve, cities will be safer and flourish again and homelessness will be addressed one way or the other. It's a win-win situation.

• The homelessness issue must be resolved at the local level by law enforcement agencies. There is no need for additional agencies; it is only a temporary need for it.

The USO (United Service Organizations)

• Many homeless individuals could volunteer for the USO. They would learn valuable skills such as building houses, electrical work, carpentry, masonry, roofing, plumbing, and other trades. They would gain discipline, work ethics, and healthier lifestyles while overcoming drugs, alcohol, and other unhealthy habits. They would become productive members of society, ready to join their families and start new lives. With their new skills, they could secure employment and avoid begging for food or money, leading to a better life and possibly even starting a family.

Ronald Reagan said: "We can't help everyone, but everyone can help someone. Let's all start doing that for a better country." Huge Corporations can jump in and help here any time, they have huge amounts of funds and then some.

• This is an opportunity of a lifetime for some of the greatest companies in the US, like SpaceX, Apple, GE, Lockheed Martin, and so many others, to help fund the USO to build housing for these American heroes veterans. This would eliminate homelessness and restore the tradition of philanthropy. The government could offer tax credits to companies for their contributions, helping Americans in need and improving the country. America would be safer, more beautiful, and a source of pride for all of us. This is my dream for America: to proudly sing "America the Beautiful" again.

• Some of these individuals could even be recruited by the US military. The military could provide direction, discipline, and new career opportunities for homeless young men and women. It will take time, but it will be worth it, saving many young souls in the process. Again, it's a win-win situation.

Henry Ford said it best: **"If everyone is moving forward together, then success takes care of itself."**

On Welfare

I totally understand that some people go through hard times for various reasons. For myself, I have been working since I was 15 years old. Even when my family relocated to the beautiful United States of America, I was never without a job for more than a few days. NEVER. When we arrived here, just five days later, I started working on the assembly line. I didn't speak more than 20 words of English, but I didn't need to. They showed me what to do, and I was more than happy to do it. Yes, it was minimum wage, but so what? I HAD A JOB in America. I went to school, learned English, and found a new job with better pay. And so on. NO ONE in my family ever received money for nothing. We all worked, and we were very proud to be here working. Now, looking back at my life, I am shocked at how much this beautiful country, the USA, has changed, and how people have changed. Most people want something for nothing. They think that America OWES them a living or something. How wrong they are. The only thing America owes them is SAFETY.

President John F. Kennedy once said it best. He inspired children and adults alike. Here it goes: ***"Ask not what your country can do for you—ask what you can do for your country."***

People should be reminded of this more often. President Donald Trump should remind people of what John F. Kennedy said. He was an American Patriot also. People were Inspired then and they can be inspired again today. If anybody can say it right, then President Donald Trump can say it BEST.

On that note, I would like to say that NO able human being should be given a single red cent for NOTHING. Find a way, get a job, whatever that might be—paint a house, do handy work, be your own boss, cut grass, whatever. But be proud and make your family proud. WORK. If that is not enough, then some church or organization (maybe government-sponsored) should provide you and your family with a kitchen where you can go and eat. NEVER MONEY and/or DEBIT CARDS or Smartphones.

Remember: **"Dreaming is achieving."** Dream big. Someone once said that if your dream came true, you did not dream big enough. If you dream, DREAM BIG.

God Bless America and us all to be able to right the American ship for a bright and beautiful future.

SOCIAL SECURITY

• Social Security is collecting billions of dollars in taxes every year from illegal immigrants with fraudulent Social Security cards. What is being done with all this money? The government knows that this money is collected illegally. They are supposed to operate within the law at all times and set an example for us. Does anyone in Congress know what is happening with these huge amounts of money? The public has the right to know what happens to these billions of dollars.

• It is both illegal and immoral for Congress to divert money from Social Security funds for any reason whatsoever. The system was set up to protect these funds. Money is supposed to be invested and brought in a lot of extra money in the form of PROFIT. Now all our money is gone and they, the Congress, are talking about the system crashing in just a few more years. This is unacceptable. We demand that the money be put back somehow. You wasted our money, you figured it out. Whatever will take, we demand PUT IT BACK. Now Social Security is going broke because Congress has failed to restore the funds, plus interest.

• Many immigrants bring their retired parents from their country of origin to the U.S. Within days of their arrival, these parents are taken to a Social Security office to apply for benefits, often receiving around $1,000 per person per month or even more. This is in addition to what they collect from their country of origin. Moreover, they also receive Medicare or Medicaid benefits, which include free operations and other services, costing tens of thousands of dollars. Where does this money come from? The answer is: from hard-working Americans who pay high taxes, including Social Security and unemployment taxes. Social Security Services are giving our money away as if it were their personal funds. It is not their right to give money to illegals or to people who have never worked in this country. Again Social Security Services is acting in a very illegal way. It's downright Criminal. They are stealing our money. At least these people should be fired right away and lose all their benefits.

• People who come here on a green card or tourist visa are sponsored and legally responsible for, by their family or friends. They sign legal papers to that effect with the American government. So why are Social Security employees not asking these system cheaters for the right documents and reporting them to the INS? No wonder Social Security is going broke among other reasons. This insanity must STOP immediately.

• I know several people who worked as entrepreneurs, barely making a living. After 30, 40, or 50 years of hard work, they only receive $475 per month from Social Security. Is this right? No. On one hand, we have individuals who worked hard for over 50 years in the U.S. and receive $475 per month. On the other hand, a person who just arrived in the U.S. can receive over $1,000 per month plus free medical benefits. This is wrong. How can this be right? It is not right and needs to be fixed. The people who sponsored their families are responsible for fulfilling their promise to the American government and taking care of these individuals, or, if they can't afford it, sending them back. Period. Goodbye.

• This problem needs to be fixed quickly. First, new leadership is required at Social Security Services, not just at the top but down through about five levels. Salaries and benefits should be reviewed, and pension plans should be adjusted to be lower than what we receive in private industries. We work harder and produce income for the country, paying taxes to cover these salaries. It's only fair.

ISRAEL VS. HAMAS

● Israel is fighting Hamas, which is not a country but a militant Palestinian Islamist political party. Most countries recognize Hamas as a terrorist group, and it is sponsored by Iran—a fact widely known. Hamas set up operations in Gaza, where most people are Palestinian. Hamas operates with impunity, using women, children, and hospitals as human shields and embezzling millions of dollars from Palestinians. They use most of the money to acquire arms, bombs, and other resources for terrorism against Israel. Other Iranian-sponsored terrorist organizations include Hezbollah in South Lebanon, the Houthis in Yemen, Al-Shabaab in Somalia, Islamic Jihad, and Kata'ib Hezbollah in Iraq. All of these organizations take orders from the Iranian government and the Revolutionary Guards. Hamas receives substantial support from Iran, including armament, ammunition, intelligence, and equipment for constructing tunnels and carrying out terrorist acts against Israel. In October 2023, Hamas committed brutal, inhumane, and cowardly acts of terror.

• Following the Hamas terrorist attack on Israel, 1,200 innocent people were killed, hundreds were wounded, and 252 were taken hostage. Some hostages were beaten, raped, mutilated, and killed. In response, Israeli Prime Minister Benjamin Netanyahu decided that Israel must eliminate Hamas. Just as President Donald Trump, did the right thing to protect Americans, and decisively destroyed the ISIS Caliphate that threatened the U.S., Israel has the right to take similar action against Hamas, Hezbollah, and other groups that threaten its integrity, way of life, and security.

• Iran must also be held accountable for financing and supplying these terrorist groups with money, armament, and other resources that enable them to conduct barbaric acts of terror and cause chaos in the region.

• Destroy Hamas, Hezbollah, and all terrorist groups in Yemen, Somalia, or anywhere else they exist. The world will be a better place without them. Any new terrorist groups must be dealt with immediately. They must be taken out as soon as possible. No more delays.

• The region will be much more stable.

• The next step is to destroy all of Iran's military facilities, including military airports, military bases, armament factories, and nuclear facilities. This would cripple the Iranian government for at least 25 years, if not forever.

• Next, Iran should be isolated from the rest of the world by blocking all its money and assets globally. No commerce should occur between Iran and any UN member until the Iranian people overthrow the Ayatollahs' government and the Revolutionary Guards and establish a new government that provides

freedom of speech, freedom of religion, and quality education for all. Have a treaty of friendship with Israel. This is the only way to achieve peace in the area. As President Ronald Reagan said, "Peace through strength."

• I hope the people of Iran will soon have a strong leader to help them replace the Islamic government with a government of the people and for the people.

• Because there is ONLY one way to keep the peace, " President Ronald Reagan said; Peace Through Strength."

TAXES

Federal Income Tax, State Income Tax, Property Tax, Social Security Tax, Medicare Tax, Insurance Policies Tax, Unemployment Tax, Consumption Tax, Retail Tax, Value Added Tax, Excise Tax, Luxury Tax, and don't forget the Death Tax. You work all your life, maybe able to put aside a little money or a lot—it doesn't matter. One day, you die, and guess what? The Government will come knocking and demand from your children to pay taxes on the little nest egg you left behind. The same nest egg you've already paid tons of taxes on over your lifetime. WHY, WHY? This is just insane. I have never realized we are paying so many types of taxes. It's not right; it's time for a change.

The American Revolution

It was all about taxation without representation. The English Empire was demanding 2% in taxes, and the Americans decided to go it alone, hence the independence. Now we've slowly allowed a government infested with crooked politicians to destroy American values and the American Dream, and they're doing this at the point of a gun. Try not paying any of these taxes—I dare you. They take our money at higher and higher rates. Now up to 50% or more of our hard-earned money. What the hell happened to us? How did we allow the Government to do this to us? From 2% to 50%, and we still elect this bunch of professional crooks to rule us. It's time to take back our government. Revolt, by VOTE. Elect public servants who are of the people and for the people—people who truly love America and its people, who are willing to serve us and not themselves. TIME FOR A BIG CHANGE. VOTE for President Donald Trump, a true American Hero.

This is what our politicians are doing to us. It is outrageous and even downright criminal. I believe that all taxes, IRS and state, must be reformed. All other taxes must be stopped and included in the State tax and IRS tax. Are you with me? We pay way too much and get back very little. Money is misused and stolen at all levels. I think that all taxes should be redone and approved by the people, but only after the size of the government has been drastically reduced. There should be only two types of taxes: state and federal. Once you pay the income tax to the state and federal government, you will know how much is left and how to budget yourself. The law should be such that it can never be changed except to increase the inflation index. A flat tax might be even better, ensuring everyone pays their fair share. This applies to both personal income tax and corporations, small and large. Fair share.

I don't know what other countries are doing with taxes, and I don't care. We are in the United States of America, and I care very much about what happens here to all of us. I do care very much about how much the state and federal governments are forcing us to pay year after year, more and more, from our hard-earned money. Every year, they invent more ways to take our money. They are very good at this. I'm willing to bet they've hired many people just to figure out how to take more money from us, the American people. They sneak into our back pockets and take whatever they want. It used to be that all government employees worked for us. Not true anymore. We work for them and work very hard. Government people are not just a few, oh NO. There are over 3.5 million of them.

There are a lot of people and their families, doing nothing that we have to feed every year. They make more money than you and I, more benefits than you and I, and a hell of a pension plan that you and I DON'T have. Time for us to stand up and demand that the Government be cut down to what it was 100 years ago, per capita. Get ready for all the dead wood. We need workers in the private industries, a lot of them. Find a job, join us, the working class. See what it is like to actually earn a living. We pay our income tax every year, and even there, they figure out how to add new taxes and more taxes on what we have left. We work six to eight months per year just to pay taxes. And then when we die they take even more of our money that we already. paid a ton of taxes. This just isn't fair to any of us. A total annual tax of 20% yes, I can see that, but not a penny more, I don't mind that. But anything more is highway robbery. We are just getting killed, There is NO MORE middle class. We are all poor, living week to week, that is the reality.

Let me tell you this: In California, on June 6, 1978, the people of California, led by a man named Howard Jarvis, revolted against the government of California (it was a "Revolt by Vote") for taxing them out of their houses. Proposition 13 passed by a landslide. Basically, Proposition 13 slashed property taxes from 2.67% to 1% per year and significantly limited how much they could increase and how often. That was a huge reduction in taxes and helped the residents of California immensely. But now, property taxes are still 1% of the purchase price. However, there are additional local tax rates, exemptions, garbage taxes, and many others. Also, voter-approved bond taxes, fees, and special taxes. How do you like this? They found a way around to add extra taxes. This should NOT be possible.

Now, I would like to know: if we pay our income tax every week via payroll check, there should be only two types of deductions every week: federal income tax and state tax. But that is not it. There are many other deductions: Social Security, Medicare taxes, insurance policies, unemployment taxes, retirement, and other payroll withholdings. Got it? And if that's not bad enough, you take home whatever is left —maybe 50%—and think, "OK, I have to live with this." But you would be dead wrong. Because as soon as you go out shopping, to restaurants, to movies, or try to spend any money in any way, shape, or form, there they are again. They have people from all walks of life collecting more taxes for them. Try consumption tax, retail tax, value-added tax, excise tax, and other taxes. After paying all these other taxes, tell me, how much do you have left in your pocket? 20%? 25%, if you're lucky?

This is why people can't get ahead anymore. And this is not all. Wait a minute, banks are also at your door asking for their cut. What interest do you pay on your precious Mastercard or Visa? Do you know? 25%? 29.99%? American citizens are struggling from week to week. We can never live the American Dream anymore. It was squashed a long time ago, taken from us ever so slowly, one dollar at a time. We did not see it coming. In the 1970s, I was a new immigrant to this country working for minimum wage. That first year, I made around $9,000 and changed. Eight months later, I bought a brand-new GM car, one of the best, for about $4,800. That was half of my minimum salary that year. Try that today. FORGET IT. Three years later, I bought my first two-story house and paid less than $30,000. The upstairs renters were paying me almost the whole mortgage payment. I had to add approximately $50 a month from my pocket. That was the American Dream. I lived it. Life was so beautiful and plentiful. Where did it all go? Ask your hungry and greedy politicians.

Why is this? It's called GREED. Yes, GREED. We work for the first 6-8 months of the year just to pay State and IRS and all the other taxes. I have mentioned the banks—don't forget the banks. They, the politicians, and the banks are getting fat on our backs, at the cost of our families and children. There is NO MORE AMERICAN DREAM. But I believe we can have it again. I believe, with God's help, President Donald Trump is the most Patriotic American since Abraham Lincoln. We can turn this country around. The first step: VOTE for President Donald Trump. Then he MUST clean the government. Vote out every politician who has been in office for more than 12 years. I don't care who they are. Get New and American Patriots in there. Every federal duplicate department that every state has already MUST be closed at once—no exceptions. Let the states do their job. Their people know better what is good for them, not the DC bureaucrats. Over 3.5 million of them. Redo and reduce all taxes. A FLAT tax would be best for individuals and corporations. This way, all of us are paying our fair share.

People ran to America to escape the English Empire. WHY, you may ask? To escape the king taxing without representation. 2% tax. This, my dear American patriots, is exactly what is happening to us now. It must be STOPPED, and it must be STOPPED now before it's too late. Personally, I think we are already too late. But we have no place to run now, so what are we supposed to do? We have to have our peaceful revolution " Revolt, by Vote." We MUST fix our country. Get rid of the far-left extremists, the American haters, and the communist elite. NO MORE TYRANNY. Let us all VOTE for a new beginning. GOD be with us.

The great President John F. Kennedy said, *"If you make peaceful revolution impossible, you make violent revolution inevitable."*

A Little Reality Check on Why the Taxes Are So High

• This is what I found out: In 1933, our population was just over 125 million people. At that time, the total number of federal government employees was around half a million, which translates to one federal employee per 250 citizens. Right after Franklin Roosevelt's third term presidency, government employment shot up to over 3.5 million bureaucrats, even though this was during World War II. These are crazy numbers. To his credit, or perhaps Harry Truman's, the numbers decreased drastically after the war was over. I did not find exact numbers, but that's not important. But today with all these technologies there should be one per 500 Citizens. They don't have to chase files down from some basement anymore. They make all the changes from their desks.

• By 2023, there were approximately just over 3.5 million federal employees, equating to one federal employee for every 95 citizens. It should be one per 500 Citizens. It worked great then, and it can work even better today with the help of computers and AI. In my opinion, it should be even more than one per 500 citizens, especially with all the new technologies. It is wrong for so many millions of people to be supported by the rest of us. How do you feel about this? Revolt, by Vote.

• Why is it that we treat illegal immigrants better than our war veterans, many of whom are homeless? As of 2023, the rate of veteran homelessness is at 35.57%. What a shame for our country and for all of us. We stand by, doing nothing. These young men, now grown men, gave up their youth to serve the USA. They went to war in foreign countries, far from home and their loved ones, sometimes for months or years at a time. They fought there, got hurt, lost limbs, and worse, came back with severe mental health issues or didn't return at all. When they come home, instead of being received like the heroes, that they are, as it used, they are ignored by everybody, especially our own Government. Where are the patriotic TV stations we used to have? Shame on them all. Fake News, They couldn't care less about these Veterans. They are too busy coming up with lies about

President Donald Trump. And if not that, then too busy spreading Propaganda

• These events should be covered regularly. Our citizens and children should know who these veterans are and appreciate what it takes to have our freedoms. Freedom is not free. Our government is ignoring them, leaving them homeless and without proper help. President Trump tried to fix many of the wrongs, and although he is a great man and patriot, where was the rest of his team? President Biden has undone everything President Trump did for our veterans, the American HEROES. Hopefully, this time around, President Trump won't have as many snakes pretending to work with him, as he did the first time. They constantly sabotaged his efforts. Paul Ryan is one of the biggest snakes in the history of American politics. I'm sure he learned his lesson. You know what they say: "Screw me once, shame on you; screw me twice, shame on me."

• I think Jim Jordan should be the Speaker of the House. He is a true American patriot, and I believe he would make a great team player with President Trump.

• Anyway, my point is that these great heroes of ours should receive the very best care available. No one should be left to chance. We should keep in touch with every one of them, help them rehabilitate, and, if possible, reintegrate them into society productively. Put them in four- and five-star hotels if necessary and send the illegals back to their home countries. No debit cards, no phones, and no benefits for the illegals. All these benefits should go to our men and women veterans, the true heroes. They are a special breed of people who were ready to give up their lives for this great country, the USA. God bless them all and their families.

● Ronald Reagan said: *"We can't help everyone, but everyone can help someone. Let's all start doing that for a better country."*

US CITIZENSHIP

John F. Kennedy once said: ***"Ask not what the country can do for you—ask what YOU can do for your country."***

I believe that every boy and girl should undergo a minimum of one year of military training by the age of 21. This could be three months every summer during high school, or if not, immediately after high school. We live in a crazy world today and all of us must be prepared for anything. Thanks to many unwise politicians, we have made many lots of enemies over the years.

In Israel, boys are required to have 36 months of military training and girls 23 months. So, one year is nothing and does not interfere with school or other important activities. Freedom is NOT free. "Everybody has to have some skin in the game," they say. It's a dangerous world out there, with criminals loose in every city. Our kids are in grave danger wherever they go. They must learn self-defense.

American kids MUST understand the USA and its history, what it means to be a US citizen, including the benefits and responsibilities. They should learn the Constitution to prevent misinformation and to understand their responsibilities, including voting. They need to be educated about our great history.

Citizenship should ONLY be awarded to babies born on US soil to women who are American citizens. NO EXCEPTIONS.

Citizenship should NOT be awarded to individuals before they can speak at least semi-fluently in English, understand the history of the United States, and have a solid grasp of the political system and the Constitution. Citizenship MUST be applied for during the first week after the five-year anniversary of receiving the Green Card. How can they vote if they are not US citizens and do not understand the system? If they do not want American citizenship, then we DON'T want them. Ship them out, PRONTO.

A year after I arrived in the USA, I spoke a little English but not well enough to work at the airport where I would have liked to work. Of course, I was turned down because I didn't speak English fluently and was not yet an American citizen. I was very disappointed, but I understood. Sensitive jobs like this should ONLY be given to American citizens, and I would add, to NATURALLY BORN American citizens. Too many naturalized American citizens today are not entirely loyal to the United States. I would vet very carefully such citizens and not allow them any sensitive government jobs. American-born citizens should come first.

NO foreigners from aggressive or non-friendly countries toward America should be allowed to attend state or federally-funded colleges and universities, or even private institutions, NO EXCEPTIONS. The same applies to IT, research, aerospace, or any other areas sensitive to national security.

I love and believe in America. DO YOU? If your answer is NO, do us all a favor. GET OUT as fast as you can; we won't mind. Go anywhere else—Canada, Mexico, or maybe you'd prefer China. Personally, I wish you nothing but the BEST.

Thomas Jefferson once said: *"A government afraid of its citizens is a DEMOCRACY. Citizens afraid of the government are TYRANNY."*

On Protests

Any student protesting against the United States in support of Hamas or any other terrorist organization or enemy country should be arrested and have their citizenship and visa status checked. Those with student visas, temporary visas, green cards, or even naturalized citizens should be deported to their country of origin immediately and barred from returning to the US, even as visitors. They should also be placed on the No Fly List indefinitely. Their citizenship and green cards should be revoked. Students with American citizenship by birth should have their right to vote removed for 12 years and be barred from attending any university or higher education institution for the rest of their lives. Period. If we are not firm with these individuals, they will continue to undermine us. This is not freedom of speech; it is anarchy when they infringe on our rights.

On National Anthem

• From K through 12, the National Anthem must be sung at the beginning of the first class every day. It is a MUST and non-negotiable. We need to teach our kids to be proud Americans and what it means to be an American—no exceptions. Make it the law of the land. If anyone is offended, they should be shipped out of the country and never allowed back; put them on the no-fly list. End of discussion. This kind of behavior sets a bad example for our kids. These people are not Patriots.

• Americans who refuse to sing the National Anthem for any reason should have their right to vote revoked—no excuses. We have become too accommodating to those who come to this country either to exploit it or, worse, to harm the United States and our way of life.

• We have people in this country who have lived here for years and still do not speak English. Shame on them. I would immediately stop printing any government documents in any language other than English. When I came to the US in the early '70s, everything was printed in English only. If they want to stay here, they MUST learn English to assimilate—no excuses. All states and the American government spend billions of dollars every year printing forms in multiple languages and providing translators for millions of people. CUT IT OFF. If they refuse to learn English in three years, again, OUT THEY GO.

GREAT BLACK LEADERS OF AMERICA UNITE

Some wisdom from the great J.C. Watts, a former Football Player who spent 8 years in the US House of Representatives from 1995-2003. Oklahoma. He said; " *I embrace my blackness, just as I do my conservatism and my Christianity, but I don't want to be defined or pigeonholed by any one of the many elements that make up my character.* "

We do well to remember some of our history. The Democrats were the ones who supported slavery. They fought for slavery during the Civil War, which was the main cause of that conflict. How many Americans died in that war? 620,000 people, which was 2% of the entire population of the USA at that time. Wow. But thanks to President Abraham Lincoln, they won their freedom.

When the Emancipation Act of 1838 was put to vote, every Republican Voted YES and every Democrat Voted NO. Get It/

The Democrats were also responsible for creating the KKK. How many innocent Black people were lynched by the KKK? Robert Byrd, a respected Democrat Senator for 51 years, was once a Grand Wizard of the KKK. In 1940, he organized and led a local chapter of the KKK and filibustered against the Civil Rights Act in 1964. NOT Republicans—DEMOCRATS. REMEMBER THAT WHEN YOU VOTE ON NOVEMBER 5TH, 2024.

There are so many great Black leaders among us today. I wish they would form a coalition to challenge the Democrats for using Americans of color as pawns, without ever planning to actually help them. Demand to know why the biggest drug problems, lack of education, and lack of employment are in their neighborhoods. Why do they let the Democrats get away with their UGLY past?

This group of great Black Americans should advocate for Black American kids across the country. Use their fame and influence to make things right. Demand new and better schools. Teach young men and women the importance of the family unit and the enormous need for children to have a dad and a mom at home. For men to take responsibility and be present in raising the kids, it pays off later in life. When they get older they will realize this and they will be very happy. Our children are the ones who will help us in our later years. It's beautiful. We need to teach them the true American history and the history of the Democrats. Understand who did what. It takes a lot of education for these values to sink in. We can never give up on this, no matter what. Start with the youngest and never stop. It is WORTH it. America will be much better off with the new generation of very well-educated kids. A great education is where the true value is in us, all of us, You should demand much better schools and better teachers. Ask for help, go visit President Donald Trump, he WILL help you.

Ben Carson is another amazing and wonderful man—a true PATRIOT. He is highly accomplished, and respected, and it's a pleasure to listen to him. He worked with President Donald Trump in his first term, and I hope he will seize the opportunity to work with President Trump again to help our young Black and beautiful kids across the country get the same opportunities as any other child. I know he is only one man, but what a man. He will know what to do.

There are many wonderful black individuals who have lived the American Dream: Denzel Washington, Samuel L. Jackson, Condoleezza Rice, Candace Owens, Alan Keyes, Larry Elder, J.C. Watts, football legend Lynn Swann, T.D. Jakes, Clarence Thomas, and many, many others. Form an organization for this purpose, get very active, and help them achieve the American Dream. Demand that our politicians make the necessary changes now, not later. Don't take NO for an answer. All of you should meet with President Trump; he will help you make it happen. This is the right time if there ever was one. Don't waste it. Just think about the huge difference a group of such accomplished individuals can make. Teach these kids to believe in themselves and that they CAN be anything they want. Just as you have believed all your life. Most of these kids grew up without a father, maybe in the streets. They need a father figure to get guidance and convince them to a great education. But to do that they need new schools. In the afternoon a place to unwind, the typical places we used to go to when we grew up. They should also attend summer camps, a great place to learn about life, responsibility, and family. They can have a wonderful life if we offer them a safe environment and a good education system. A charter school system, not the inadequate options available in today's Public Schools. We all know about the quality of most Public Schools. Get together with President Trump as soon as he has won the election. Don't waste any time. It can be done. Don't rest; don't delay. Our enemies never rest. Then we can not afford to rest either. JUST DO IT. Give these kids a new chance to have a better life. Great for everybody.

On Poverty

I challenge prominent citizens like Magic Johnson, Elon Musk, Jeff Bezos, and many others who are exceptionally wealthy and fortunate to form charities specifically for the less fortunate. Take control of these charities and help those who are truly struggling to support their families but lack the resources to succeed. We are very different from one another, but we can make a difference by extending a helping hand.

I am not advocating giving something for nothing. On the contrary, to qualify for assistance, individuals would need to be free of drugs, alcohol, and any other detrimental substances or behaviors. We should create ways to teach these individuals new skills. Consider placing them in companies to learn a trade or enrolling them in specialized trade schools to support them and their families.

The adage goes, "**Give a man a fish, and you feed him for a day. Teach a man to fish, and you feed him for a lifetime.**"

By providing education and guidance, these individuals can become richer happier, and better members of society. This approach will be highly satisfying and make your life feel more complete. Your blessings will multiply a thousandfold. Remember, we are all God's children. Together, we can make America a much better place. No more handouts—we've tried that for over 60 years, and it didn't work. Let's return to traditional methods of work cooperation and **Philanthropy.** We can **Make America Great Again** for ourselves, our children, and future generations. Under President Donald Trump's leadership, America can turn in the right direction, united and prosperous. God bless the people of America and President Trump, for the next thousand years.

Additionally, we should fight for those who want to work but can't find jobs due to millions of illegal immigrants taking positions for half the pay. Companies that hire illegal immigrants should be required to fire them and face hefty fines.

President Donald Trump should demand (not ask) that establishment politicians in both houses of Congress pass a bill to create charter schools, ensuring that all children receive a great education, equal to any in the country. Families should receive vouchers to send their children to any school of their choosing, including private schools. The only way out of gangs and poverty is through a great education. Our greatest treasure is our children. We need to create the best school system ever. The future will be brighter for our children and our country. When will politicians understand this? More education equals a greater treasure. So, teach, teach, and teach. Make it better.

John Wooden once said, **"Be more concerned with your character than your reputation, because your character is what you really are, while your reputation is merely what others think you are."**

IMMIGRATION

• Over the last 35 years, the number of illegal immigrants in the US, specifically Mexicans, has increased by more than 15-fold. By 2004, there were approximately 11 million illegals in the US, with an average yearly growth of 8%. Trying to determine how many illegal immigrants have come to the US in the last four years is impossible. We know for sure that it practically exploded after President Biden took office. Just from the news and my estimates, I would say more than 10 million people have crossed illegally into the USA since President Biden took office. Today, it is estimated there are over 30 million illegals in America. How accurate are these numbers? No one knows yet. No one is talking. Maybe after President Trump takes office again for his second term, we will find out.

It is absolutely inhumane what President Biden has done with all the laws that were in place by 2020. All these people trying to cross the border are getting hurt, raped, or worse, killed—all because President Biden signaled that anyone could come in. Not one person was vetted.

Countries from South America, drug dealers, and gangs of the worst kind, as well as crazies from asylums, Africa with many terrorists, Asia including China with spies and some terrorists, and the Middle East with most being terrorists—hundreds of thousands of them are now in all our states and cities. Only God knows what will happen in the near future. We already see a rise in rapes, burglaries, and various crimes.

Illegals also place a huge strain on public resources such as hospitals, schools, and other social services. They receive debit cards and smartphones and even stay in 4 and 5-star hotels while our veterans sleep on the streets. We know well that this will eventually lead to higher taxes.

Health concerns are significant because many of these illegals come here very sick with transmittable diseases like Tuberculosis, Hepatitis, and various STDs.

• Job competition: Illegals work for much less money and without insurance, benefits, or paying taxes. This is a huge drawback for our young people who want to work and can't find jobs. Many places now won't hire you if you don't speak

Spanish, which is discrimination and happens all the time in the Southern states. But, of course, no one cares.

- Finish the wall ASAP.

- Deport all illegal immigrants as soon as they are caught.

- Stop all benefits to illegal immigrants, including their anchor babies, and revoke the babies' citizenship if their mothers were here illegally.

- Fine companies $100,000 per illegal immigrant they hire, per year.

- Deport all illegal immigrant criminals to their country of origin ASAP. Perhaps make a deal with El Salvador's President Nayib Bukele; I hear he built a large, beautiful prison. It will be much cheaper.

EQUALITY

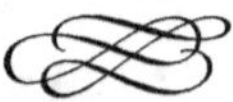

"Here Are the Values That I Stand For: Honesty, equality, kindness, compassion, treating people the way you want to be treated, and helping those in need. To me, those are traditional values." — Ellen DeGeneres, comedian and actress.

• Promoting equality is very important to us all. It creates a more fair and just society. We are all entitled to equal rights, opportunities, and value. We seek non-discrimination, fairness, and justice for all.

• The idea is that all people, regardless of color, religion, or any other characteristic, should be given opportunities to achieve their goals, whatever they may be.

• We are all God's people, but we are not all the same. Thank God for that. If we were all alike, life would be very boring.

● God gave us different talents, so we must discover what those talents are. We need to find out what we are good at and what makes us happy. That is what makes life and us all beautiful.

●   The French say **"Vive la différence,"** meaning appreciation of diversity. We have the capacity to make our own decisions about what we want to do, where we want to go, and where we want to live. It is a beautiful thing.

● We also have the right to make decisions for ourselves, including how much we want to work or just maybe, how much we dislike to work. Hey, you know what they say " Different strokes for different folks."

● America, like the rest of the world, was never perfect and never will be. But the important thing is that we are always trying to do better, although sometimes too slowly, thanks to incompetent politicians. The more pressure we put on our politicians, the faster progress will be made. Unfortunately, we must vote out most of our politicians. They are too old and unwilling to change. As they say, **"You can't teach an old dog new tricks."** I say, **"Revolt, by Vote."** Vote them out after 12 years on the job. These politicians are living in the past. We need smart, young, qualified Americans eager to help shape a new, better America for us, our kids, and future generations. Join the **MAGA** movement; it's a beautiful thing.

• This is the opportunity of the century. Let Us Take it from here. M.A.G.A. all the way.

GOVERNMENT SUBSIDIES

• No business, big or small, should be subsidized by the government. Government loans might be acceptable if backed by collateral, but outright subsidies are not. It's unfair that huge companies like GE, Boeing, Northrop Grumman, and many others that make substantial profits, into the billions, Year after year, do not pay any taxes and, on top of that, receive enormous welfare checks from federal and state governments, amounting to billions of dollars. This is unfair to those of us who pay significant amounts in taxes.

• Let the market take care of itself. Subsidizing businesses means the government is playing favorites. Big farming corporations receive billions of dollars in subsidies every year, while small farmers go bankrupt. This is not right. The land belongs to the small farmers who have been feeding

America for decades. Big corporations are destroying the land with their focus on money, and their greed is harming us all in the long run. Synthetic fertilizers, pesticides, antibiotics, and steroids are poisoning us and our children. We are becoming overweight, obese, and sick with numerous diseases. This is what America has become. Who will stop this catastrophe? Not our run-of-the-mill politicians, they don't know a cow from a hole in the ground. They are only interested in money. This November 5th, 2024, vote them out. Make it right. I'm not saying all politicians are bad, but a majority certainly are. Especially the ones who have been in there for more than 12 years. They don't believe in MAGA. **"REVOLT, by VOTE."**

• Big farm corporations seem to produce much lower quality food compared to the produce from family farmers. People across America are increasingly suffering from various diseases. Imports of food must be banned unless the products are organic. Additionally, if we care about the environment, all chemicals must be banned from production and use. These products are not only harmful to the environment but also deadly to humans, birds, and animals.

• At a hearing in 1984, Congressman Stewart McKinney said, "We have a new kind of bank. It's called **"TOO BIG TO FAIL."** (Thank you, President Bush.) In other words, it's a monopoly. When a business is at the point of insolvency, the government should take over and order the company or bank to be sold as quickly as possible, preferably in smaller pieces. Why throw good money after bad? There are many companies with lots of money and numerous billionaires looking for investments. Let them buy parts of these failing Companies / Banks. They will make it right. No public money should be used. However, entities from anywhere in the world considered aggressive towards America, enemy states, like China, Iran, Russia, or Terrorist states should not be allowed to buy anything in the United States. EVER.

WEAPONIZATION OF NSA, FBI, DOJ, IRS, AND STATE DEPARTMENT

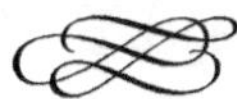

- The weaponization of the State Department, NSA, DOJ, IRS, FBI, and other government departments became glaringly obvious last year in their actions against President Donald Trump. They don't even try to hide it anymore; they do it on purpose **to intimidate us, the American Citizens.** If they can target an ex-president like Donald Trump, imagine what they could do to ordinary citizens like the majority of us. **The message is, to be afraid.** Most state and federal employees today are Democrats. It took years for them to gain this control and vote in block for the Democrats. They secure millions of guaranteed votes from this block, both at the State and Federal Levels. They act with impunity because no one dares to challenge them for their crimes against the American people. You get no cooperation from these people; otherwise, they would lose their jobs. They cover for each other. Time to stand up and make a difference, are you ready? MAGA!!!

• These departments must be rebuilt from the ground up. Real, good people, American patriots, should be put in charge of each department and rebuilt as soon as possible.

• The treatment of President Donald Trump since he announced his candidacy in 2015, including the recent four indictments on over 90 charges, is an absolute **crime**. We have lost control of our country and have become a police state, a tyrannical state. When you are afraid to speak your mind in Public, in the streets, or in Restaurants you know we are in trouble. Freedom of speech is gone. You have House of Representative members, like Maxim Waters no less, calling on TV and other means of Social Media other democrats that hear us or recognize us anywhere to start harassing and make us leave whatever establishment we are in. This is not only hate speech but much, much more than that. This is calling for unrest. This is so wrong on so many levels that it is not funny. If there was a Republican calling for this he would be in Prison by the next day. We are afraid to speak out in public anymore. If we express our opinions, we risk vandalism of our cars and homes. We cannot sit on the sidelines any longer. Our freedom of speech is gone in major cities controlled by Democrats. Revolt, by voting this woman out of Congress, she does NOT belong there anymore if she ever was.

• This situation is terrifying. The future belongs to the US, not to them. NOT TO THEM. It is time to stand up and make a difference. Save our country from these communists and American haters. They are the **enemy within.** Don't forget this applies to both Democrats and Republicans alike. If they've been in office for more than 12 years, vote them out.

• Even some of the Democrats, like Robert Kenedy Jr., do not agree with what is happening in this country. Many Democrats already jumped ship to the Republican's side. Let's unite and vote for America's future. Vote for President Donald Trump and the Republican Party. I promise you will be glad you voted for the betterment of our beautiful country, The United States of America, not just the party. And don't vote for anyone who has been in office for more than 12 years. It's really time for new blood in both houses of Congress.

• With God's help, through President Donald Trump, we can right the ship. Every accusation against Mr. Trump must be investigated. They interfered with the 2024 Election Process. That is a Federal Crime. Every perpetrator found guilty must be fired immediately, have all future government benefits forfeited, and, depending on the crime, may even be sent to jail. They cannot be allowed to go unpunished. The fullest extent of the law must be used. These individuals are on the verge of taking full control of our government and country. They must answer for their actions. If we don't hold them accountable, they will return and try again, and President Trump won't be there to save us. America as we know it could become history. Let's get rid of these cockroaches while we can, never to return. If they could, they'd even change the name of the USA to the United Social States of America. ENOUGH IS ENOUGH.

• We can no longer afford to be indifferent. We must get up and vote. "Revolt, by Vote." Regardless of how far ahead President Trump may be, we still must vote. Don't forget 2020. According to the last count, Mr. Trump had over 11 million more votes than in 2016 when he won his first term, yet we fell asleep—literally. The RNC, to be specific, was not on the ball. They were so confident of a win that they didn't monitor certain precincts, and the Democrats took advantage. It didn't help that Attorney General William Barr quit instead of staying and doing his job until the end. What a coward. But it turned out to be for the best, as President Trump now knows who the snakes are. (I love President Trump's Snake poem.) He should send a copy of this song to all the snakes who stabbed him in the back, including William Barr. I'm sure he has learned his lesson and now understands how Washington works. I hope his new cabinet will be mostly composed of business world people—great managers and people he has known and trusted for a long time—with very few politicians if necessary. Trust his instincts and run the country as a business. He is the best man for the job, even more so than before now. He learned from his mistakes now and had 4 years to figure out what he needed to do for the next 4 years and beyond. Get ready for the next President after him. Play it like a Chess Match. Prepare for it very carefully and very strategically. Please, Mr. Trump, don't leave anything to chance. The future of America is in your hands. We, the American people, put our future in your capable hands. God Bless you and your family for a long time.

• President Donald Trump is the most Patriotic American since Abraham Lincoln, bar none.

• Biden and his co-conspirators, who are responsible for the four indictments on 91 counts of criminal behavior against President Trump, should be held accountable for all the lies told to the American people and the millions of dollars spent to interfere with the November 5th, 2024 election. The worst of crimes.

• The new DOJ should get the facts and prosecute where necessary, applying the full extent of the law if guilty.

• Additionally, they should investigate figures like Eric Swalwell, Maxine Waters, Adam Schiff, Rashida Tlaib, Ilhan Omar, Jerrold Nadler, and A.O. Cortez. What a bunch of American haters, liars, and cheats and don't forget Communists. These people appeared on live TV and lied to the American people for years, claiming they had solid evidence that Donald Trump was guilty of Russian collusion. All lies. Now it has been proven that Hillary Clinton and the Democrats were guilty of all of that. This cannot go unpunished. They should all be held accountable for their crimes.

• *"The Best Way To Enhance Freedom In Other Lands Is To Demonstrate Here That Our Democratic System Is Worthy Of Emulation."* * President Jimmy Carter

• Right now I am afraid that the United States doesn't even come close to any Country trying to Emulate us. We became a big Banana Republic. With our current President who would want to be like the USA? They are all laughing at us. But for sure the next 1-2 years will turn things around and every Country will like to be like us. God bless the USA. **MAGA** for the next 50 years at least. God bless President Donald Trump.

U.S. BUDGET

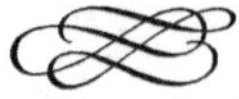

• The problem is that the Federal Government has become excessively large, with too many departments and bureaucrats. There are many duplicate departments. The United States is not a Communist country, but it certainly operates like one. According to records, there are over 3.5 million bureaucrats working for the Federal Government. Everything is centralized. Why? Every state has the right to govern itself as it sees fit, not some bureaucrat from Washington, D.C. All these departments are redundant. Billions of dollars are wasted, and these people could be productive in the private sector. Shut down all Federal Departments that exist in every State. BIG WASTE OF American Dollars. Over a trillion dollars if not more, every year.

• Eliminate all federal departments that states already have at the state level, such as the Department of Education and the Department of Public Health. There is no reason to waste billions of dollars on these departments. They are full of liars, spies for the Democrats, and worse, lazy people who haven't worked a fair day since they got their government jobs. Leave this work to each state to handle its own issues. Washington bureaucrats just make things worse. Who knows better what's good for Florida, Utah, or California than the people of those particular states?

• Get rid of all duplicate departments immediately. The U.S. budget could potentially be cut in half.

Government employees should not be allowed to have unions. Period. No government-financed pension plans. Most hard-working Americans in the private sector don't have such luxurious plans. Hard-working Americans create beautiful things like cars, rockets, and computers. They don't have government-funded pension plans. Why should government employees do this? They don't produce anything. All they do is waste money and time. Why are their average salaries almost double those in the private sector, with benefits that are excessive while people in the private market struggle to make ends meet? Government salaries should be lower (for crying out loud) than those in private industries, and their benefits should be eliminated as soon as possible.

• Make it a law that the government must have a plan in place to balance the budget within 5 years. By that time and after the budget can never exceed what is taken in. By law, NEVER. Incentivize industry to produce more in this country. They will pay more taxes, thereby generating more revenue for the government, and allowing for increased spending. working people will also generate income for the Government.

• Develop a plan and show how the United States is going to pay down the national debt. I say, like President Trump, "Drill, baby, drill" is a start. We should be able to pay our debt within 20 years maximum. Come on, we all know it is very doable. So, let's get it done already.

• The government must provide incentives for all businesses and major manufacturers to return to the United States from China within 4 years. Otherwise, significant monetary penalties should be imposed on companies that do not comply. The carrot and stick method always works. We now know for sure that **China is our worst enemy**, without question. They are out to get us, both from within and from outside. Why would the U.S. give a penny to China when we know they will use it against us?

• All manufacturers must do at least 75% of their business within the United States. No business with enemy Countries, not ever. No trade with such enemy countries either. Let other fools do it.

• It's time to take back control of this Country and be responsible for the future of this beautiful nation. Our kids, grandkids, and future generations will remember and learn about our generation and our troubles. But they will also remember the American people's **resilience**. We never give up. Never.

• Come on, President Donald Trump, make it happen! The whole world is praying for you. We are all pulling for your success. The whole world depends on the United States of America. It always has. You are the anchor of our destiny. God be with you and give you the strength to bring this job to a happy conclusion.

• *"The Basis of Our Political System is the Right of the People to Make and Alter Their Constitutions of Government."* George Washington our First Great President and Great American Patriot.

BANKS INTEREST RATES

- "A bank is a place where they lend you an umbrella in fair weather and ask for it back when it begins to rain." I don't have a clue who said this, but is true

- Banks are going crazy, and nobody seems to care. Why not? Why are banks allowed to issue credit cards to people who statistically can never pay them back? This practice is known as residual income. Banks approach their unsuspecting customers and, based on their income, offer them a credit card with a limit they believe can be managed as a minimum payment over the next few months at 1% APR. What they don't disclose is that if you miss a single payment, the interest rate jumps from 1% to a staggering 29.99%. People try to save the cards for special occasions, but before they know it, it's a kid's birthday, then Christmas, Easter, and so on. They make small purchases here and there, and by the start of the school year, the card is maxed out. Other bills pile up, and sooner or later—more likely sooner—they miss a payment.

• Now, the trap is sprung, and banks inform the unsuspecting people of the bad news. It's all there in the fine print, but it's too late to read it now. They have no choice but to make minimum payments to the bank, potentially for life. It's another form of taxation if you ask me.

• And voilà (French for "here it is"), the residual income. Millions of Americans fall into this inhumane trap. I ask again, "Where is our government protecting us?" They are too busy with insider trading, for sure. It's far more lucrative for them. Be certain that you and I would go to prison for engaging in such activity, but not them. They have a special law for themselves (made up by them, of course).

• How is it even possible? How did they manage to create a law that applies only to them? Any new law must apply to all citizens of America. Isn't that in the Constitution, that all laws must apply to everyone? Not one person in government, at any level, has challenged the banks. It seems to me that the fix is in. They have so much power that they can't even be touched, let alone stopped. An independent agency should investigate whether the banks are guilty of price fixing and other criminal behavior. They have definitely exploited the American people for years, making billions from poor and struggling fellow citizens while they live like kings. Very, very wrong. It's time to make it right. Return some of this money to your customers, quickly. A class action lawsuit might be in order. Just saying.

● ***"What we are seeing now is that greed is still alive and kicking, and banks are bigger than ever."*** Brad Pitt. It's a great one, exactly what I'm thinking. They must be cut down to size. Before you know it, they'll be too big to fail. What a bunch of thieves, them and the politicians supporting them. **Brad Pitt, you are right.**

TERRORISM AND CRIME

- I would like to start this chapter with a quote from Eleanor Roosevelt: **"It isn't enough to talk about peace; one must believe in it. And it isn't enough to believe in it; one must work at it."**

- First and of crucial importance: no names should ever be released to the public in any way, shape, or form. It should be made illegal. Anyone who breaks this law should be punished to the full extent of the law and by losing their job instantly. It's plain and simple, stupid, and only invites more criminals seeking their 15 minutes of glory to become famous or martyrs.

- In the war against terrorism, we cannot afford to trust anyone. Anyone. Got it? President Ronald Reagan used to say, "**Trust but verify.**" We must always be vigilant—always. We cannot afford to let our guard down for a second. Look at what happened to Israel on the evening of October 7th, 2023. The famous Mossad fell asleep at the wheel, and the price for Israel was very high in human lives infrastructure, and likely billions of dollars in armament.

• Terrorism comes in many forms, shapes, and colors. It's not an army. They come from all over the world, sometimes even from within. Yes, and for that, we must be connected with all friendly countries worldwide, sharing what we know and learning what they know. Only in this way can we stay a step ahead of our enemies.

• Theodore Roosevelt used to say, "**Speak softly and carry a big stick; you will go far.**"

• The war on drugs is a complete sham. We've spent billions and billions of dollars to fight drugs, but to what end? They, too, are a form of terrorism. Over the years, how far has all this money gotten us? Nowhere. Why is that? Our law on crime is a joke. The criminals, and drug dealers get arrested today and tomorrow are back in the streets again. What a **SCAM** this is !! Thousands of high-priced lawyers get filthy rich from this **WAR ON DRUGS.** Every year they are fighting and fighting, and the more they fight the richer they get. Don't you just love these kinds of war? Oh, but the lawyers do **LOVE** it. So who is writing the laws for fighting the war on drugs? Wow, you guessed it. Our politicians. You are so savvy when it comes to politics. But hold it there, what are our politicians, well most of them, **LAWYERS.** Ok, did you figure it out yet? Lawyers writing laws for Lawyers, this war will never end. **THEY DON'T WANT TO END.** Because we have a rigged and crooked system, that's why. Judges, prosecutors, and lawyers are not fighting the war on drugs to win. All they want is a piece of the action. That's a fact. The situation hasn't improved over the years; on the contrary, it has gotten much worse. There are 1.3 million lawyers alone in the U.S., and probably half of them are involved in this "war on drugs" sham. They try to get drug dealers off or make deals with the DEA to reduce sentences to a few months in jail. Out they go, free again in a few months, and the cycle starts all over. What a racket. It's a beautiful thing for them, but the process is destroying our country while judges, prosecutors, and lawyers get fat.

• Do you really want to win the war on drugs? Toughen up the laws. Look at what Singapore is doing with its drug dealers. See what they do to their prisoners in drug dealing cases after conviction: they are executed the following week. Yes, it's barbaric, but so are the people selling drugs to our kids and many adults. I'm talking about professionals too, from all walks of life. These drug users eventually end up dead from overdoses or worse. Drug addicts have no life; they become like animals, stealing, committing crimes, beating others, and destroying their families just to get another hit. They will never be able to hold another job, often ending up killed on the streets. They are killing millions of people worldwide, destroying lives, and wreaking havoc on our society, economy, labor force, and families. So do you still feel sorry for these monsters? Do you? They are also a kind of terrorist in my book. How would you feel if one of your kids, wife, or husband was affected by drugs or drug-related crimes? Just asking.

• The president of El Salvador knows how to deal with people like this. They have arrested more than 40,000 drug dealers and criminals in El Salvador alone. El Salvador used to be the country with the most murders in the world, year after year. Nayib Bukele put an end to all of this, very simply. He built a huge, beautiful prison and sent them all there to rot for the rest of their lives. That's all, and you see how they disappear. Now, El Salvador is one of the safest countries in South America. Even when you arrest drug dealers and criminals, don't put them in American prisons. Ship them straight to El Salvador where they can await their trial. Make a deal with El Salvador's president, Nayib Bukele. He will be more than happy to make a deal with us. Why pay $50,000 or more per inmate in the U.S. when he has built a brand-new, huge, beautiful prison that has housed them very comfortably for a long time?

● *"Terrorism isn't insanity. It grows out of social conditions that are well known: poverty, social oppression, dictatorship, and a void of meaning in the lives of ordinary people."* Deepak Chopra, American author and alternative medicine advocate.

RELIGIOUS REVIVAL

• ***"Every Mighty Move of the Spirit of God Has Had Its Source in the Prayer Chamber."*** E.M. Bounds

• When Donald Trump becomes president again, I hope he will invite, real soon, the best evangelists in the U.S. to the White House. I'm not sure when he can do this, given all the work at hand—maybe in a month or so. But he should ask them to help America and start a crusade movement like never before. He should invite them to come back to the White House at least a few times a year, similar to the crusades Billy Graham held throughout his life. Billy Graham was just one man and still made a huge difference in American society, for many years at the time. Imagine the impact 25 of these evangelists could have, especially in today's age of social media and large stadiums. Just think about it.

• Imagine what 25 of these great Christian leaders could accomplish if they came together. It would be the biggest Christian revival of all time. They should encourage people to attend their neighborhood churches and revive Christian family values. Sundays should be reserved for families again. We are all so busy during the week; that we need quality time with our kids and extended families. Shopping and other family business activities should be left for Monday through Saturday. It might be a bit difficult at first (it will take some planning and discipline), but we can do it. The benefits will be significant for our relationships—with our entire family and especially with our kids. Children today lack our love, guidance, discipline, support, and, most importantly, quality time. Have breakfast, lunch, and dinner together. Go to church as a family. Let kids meet other kids their age through Sunday School. They need to learn how to socialize and make friends. Nowadays, kids often hide behind their phones to avoid talking to anyone. On Sundays, all phones should stay at home. If the family goes out together, only one phone can be taken by a parent. Learn about the Lord. Singing in the choir—it's very satisfying. I know this firsthand, as I sang in the choir for many years as a kid and young adult. Do you think this will make a difference in family life? Will family relationships improve between parents and kids? Oh, yes, in a big way. GUARANTEED.

• We should encourage all businesses to close on Sundays. They will make the same amount of sales if they are all closed on Sundays. People will plan around this new schedule and have quality time with their families, getting together with other family members. I remember those times well, like in the 1970s. That's the America I remember. Now, I can hardly see the rest of my family; it's all about making money. Rush here and rush there—stress and anxiety. It never ends. We all became slaves, voluntarily. Who would have thought it? With the help of smartphones, we are on the job 24/7 and with no extra pay. Nowadays, almost everyone is for themselves. What a shame. So many missed opportunities. You can always pick up your smartphone and call, right? Forget about it. IT IS NOT THE SAME. Going to church? Forget it. I can watch it on TV or even better, on the Internet. BUT AGAIN, IT IS NOT THE SAME. You have to gather all the kids and go to church like in the old days. This way, kids will listen and learn the word of God from a young age. They will know what is right and what is wrong, learn how to respect their parents and elders, respect their country, and respect their own bodies. Our body is a temple that belongs to God. Would you throw trash into a church? They will learn the value of family. What does it take for a couple to raise a family and kids? Responsibilities. I could go on and on about this subject, but I will leave it to the evangelists.

- *"Revival Brings Back a Holy Shock to Apathy and Carelessness."* Winkie Pratney, Researcher, Author, and Communicator from New Zealand

RIOTING

● *Teddy Roosevelt used to say about foreign diplomacy: **"Speak softly, and carry a big stick."***

This is true in diplomacy, but also in the case of riots, very much so. Personally, I think this approach would also work very well in fighting drugs, crime, and terrorism. Don't you think so?

● On June 10, 2020, a violent demonstration was organized by radical left groups in Seattle, including Antifa, Black Lives Matter, and other leftist organizations. They took over buildings, blocked roads, and declared part of Seattle an Autonomous Zone. How outrageous was this?

● Violent rioters burned buildings, blocked roads, beat up people, burned cars, broke into stores, and vandalized them. Democratic leaders and the media everywhere called it a peaceful march—good citizens blowing off steam. BLOWING OFF STEAM? PEACEFUL? Really? That is exactly what they said. Bigger hypocrites you couldn't find if you tried. They didn't even attempt to stop them. How many were arrested? How many were prosecuted? Most likely NONE. What if this riot was Republican-driven?

• Martin Luther King Jr. said it best: *"Nonviolence is the answer to the crucial political and moral questions of our time; the need for mankind to overcome oppression and violence without resorting to oppression and violence."* I just wish that Antifa and Black Lives Matter would read this. As the old saying goes, **"You can catch more flies with honey than with vinegar."**

• Any students participating in protests against the United States or in support of Hamas or other terrorist groups MUST be arrested immediately. Anyone participating in these riots with any kind of visa or green card should be deported to their country of origin, and their visa and Green Cards should be revoked immediately. Also put them on the " No Fly List, indefinitely " If they are illegal immigrants, they should be deported with no chance to ever get a visa to come to the USA, also put them on "The No Fly List indefinitely." American-born students who participate should not be allowed to attend any public or private institutions of higher learning for the next 10 years. They should not be hired for any sensitive jobs. Freedom of speech comes with a huge responsibility. If we are not tough with these people, they will tear this country apart. It's as simple as that.

• All participants who broke any laws during these riots MUST be charged and prosecuted to the full extent of the law.

• Riots MUST never be allowed to develop. The police need to react immediately and put a stop to it quickly, if necessary, with the help of the local National Guard. Act swiftly. Take as many prisoners as possible and process them all. Identify the leaders of the protests if you can. Take lots of prisoners, check them out, and find out if any are known criminals. Discover who is financing these activities; they should also be held responsible.

I say to all legal immigrants who come to the U.S. Take the opportunity and "LOVE IT, RESPECT IT, OR LEAVE IT." I, for one, LOVE IT.

"The greatest challenge of the day is: how to bring about a revolution of the heart, a revolution which has to start with each one of us." Dorothy Day, American journalist and social activist.

LOBBYISTS

- *"After all, Wall Street is clearly the most powerful lobbying force on Capitol Hill. From 1998 through 2008, the financial sector spent over 5 billion dollars in lobbying and campaign contributions to deregulate Wall Street."* — Bernie Sanders

So, I say make lobbying ILLEGAL. The sooner the better.

- Lobbying should be banned forever by law. It is a grave disservice to the American people. It is all about self-service, period. Why should the very rich and powerful have even more power than they already have to manipulate the system to their advantage? When that happens, we all suffer.

- Way too many ex-politicians get rich, and some filthy rich, from such a system while the rest of us struggle more and more. This is not right, and it should be illegal forever. Follow the money, and you will see that for every decision in their favor, there is one big decision against us. If these rich and powerful people believe they have something beneficial for us all, they should take it to the public square or social media. Let the people speak up for the people.

• By definition, this means that a lobbyist is talking to a person or company, trying to promote and influence their special cause or interest with decision-makers like policymakers, politicians, or government officials. This involves direct or indirect communication with such people to convince them or change their minds on a particular issue. More often than not, such decisions are not in the public interest. Many times, illegal and/or unethical practices are used, such as bribery or even campaign finance violations. For this reason alone, since they are not working on our behalf or for our good, I strongly say MAKE IT ILLEGAL, forever.

• Just imagine that at any given time there are at least 12,000 lobbyists in Washington, D.C. Now imagine there are 100 Senators and 435 House Representatives. I would like to know, with this army of 12,000 lobbyists out there (and probably more), Knocking on their door, when do all these politicians have time to do anything else but listen to them? When do they have time to respond to our mail or even talk to us? There is no way in hell they have time for this. It is insane to have even one lobbyist. All these politicians need to spend more time talking to us, not the lobbyists. They should be in their districts, trying to solve local problems, not worrying about what special interest groups or big corporations want to get away with. All these corporations and special interest groups can go on social media or TV and take it to the people. Let the people take it up with their local politicians.

NO LOBBYISTS, NOT EVEN ONE. We, the people, don't want them. Put it to the vote and let the people decide.

• Many ex-politicians, after losing, become lobbyists, such as Nikki Haley, Rahm Emanuel, Tony Podesta, John Breaux, and many more. These lobbyists have only their special interests in mind—how to make as much money as possible while leveraging their political connections and influence. They couldn't care less about us, the American citizens. Nikki Haley, what a disappointment.

• *"In reality, everybody in Congress is a stand-in for some kind of lobbyist. In many cases, it's difficult to tell whether it's the companies that are lobbying the legislators or whether it's the other way around."* Matt Taibbi, Journalist * Man! This guy couldn't be more right. He hit the nail right on the head. Bravo.

WHITE HOUSE PRESS POOL

• Something Robin Williams said in his lifetime: *"People say satire is dead. It's not dead; it's alive and living at the White House."* How ironic, is it not?

• Every reporter seeking credentials to participate in the White House Press Pool, besides being vetted by the State Department, NSA, and FBI, should first be required to read and sign the etiquette and protocol for being in that room. First, teach them how to respect the Office of the Presidency.

• Every reporter should be allowed one question, just to keep it fair to all the other journalists in the room at the time. Think before, think hard about what you want to ask; make it count. No do-overs. No stupid questions. If someone breaks this rule, they will not be allowed to ask any questions for the next two rounds of the White House Press Pool. If they break the rule again, revoke their credentials for a year. No explanation is needed. End of discussion. Some journalists are just not smart enough to understand the rules under which they are granted credentials and have no respect for the office of the presidency.

• There are many correspondents at the White House Press Pool who are outright belligerent and obnoxious. Such people do not belong there. Kick them out, you don't have to have them there. There are plenty of good reporters there.

• *"Once you replace negative thoughts with positive ones, you'll start having positive results."* Willie Nelson, Great Country Singer (Just in case you never heard of him) Ha, Ha

THE USA FUTURE

- *"America Was Not Built On Fear. America Was Built On Courage, Imagination, And An Unbeatable Determination To Do The Job At Hand."* Harry S. Truman, 33rd US President

- To have a bright future, we MUST educate our kids, everybody, everywhere in the USA. We have to push and promote education everywhere, especially in our poor neighborhoods. Take education to the world as well. The faster we do this, the faster we'll be able to establish long-lasting peace. The more educated the Citizens are, the happier people will be. We'll be able to accomplish more and faster.

On America, the Land of Opportunity:

• America, the Land of Opportunity. Now, just imagine for a minute: America in the past was one of the greatest countries that ever existed in the world. More than 200 years later, it became the most powerful country on Earth. Probably the best and most opportune place to live anywhere. For anybody, no matter what color or religion, as long as you apply yourself and work hard, you can do it. I did it. But the American Dream is gone for now.

• Who would come to America in the past 50 years? The educated, hardworking people from Europe and all over the world came to America, hoping to make a difference in this country. This place offers an opportunity to get a new life and truly accomplish anything you can think of if you are willing to work for it. They loved it here and never looked back. They integrated with their neighbors, with America. They wanted to be Americans and they took a lot of pride in that. Many of the greatest scientists today are descendants of such immigrants. Their love for this Country and their willingness to learn got them there.

• Now, under Donald Trump's leadership, with his positive vision for business and America, and his great love for the country, America can become more powerful and productive than ever before in the next 4 to 12 years. God willing, President Trump will stay healthy and be able to implement part of his vision in the next 4 years. But that is not enough. He MUST prepare the next president after him and even the one after the next. The American people cannot leave it to chance anymore. Think ahead and stay a step ahead of the American haters and the communists. Don't even let them think that they can have a chance to power ever again.

• The American future is very bright right now. But we have to make sure that President Donald Trump wins the election. Go out PATRIOTS and VOTE, and take a friend or two with you. Volunteer to help wherever help is needed.

• With all the new technologies developing like Computers, AI, and manufacturing like SpaceX, Tesla, General Electric, Boing, General Motors and many, many more industries. Upgrading the Infrastructure This country should be booming with excitement. Bring all manufacturing back to the USA. Make the brand "**Made in USA**" a proud logo again. Just imagine where it can take us. Imagine the United States like we've never seen before. There is no end to what can be done in the United States to connect all these cities, to transport all the merchandise across the country with lightning speed. And think about what it can do for the steel industry, the glass industry, the coal industry, the concrete industry, and others. It could be amazing for the U.S. economy for years to come, with so many jobs that there won't be enough people to fill them. Legal immigration could happen in the millions just to keep up with the job demand.

This can happen now, in our lifetime. Better than ever. Thank you President Donald Trump for the hope in our future.

"The essence of living is giving" and **" Dreaming is achieving"**

author unknown. We should teach this to all of our kids from an early age and throughout their lives. The world would be a much better place. I was blessed with a mom who taught me these things throughout my childhood, and these principles have stuck with me for good. That's the reason I'm always happy. Except when I am sad. This does not happen too often though. But you must believe that dreams do come true and more importantly, work at it. Make them come true, you do have to do your part. It won't happen while you're watching TV

• "Working at it" reminds me of a joke. This guy prays to God to help him win the weekly lotto. He has been praying now for months. One night, just as he finished praying, he heard a voice from above: "For crying out loud, Johnny, go buy a ticket." It required action, you see. Do your part

• I truly believe that the American future is now, and it looks amazingly and fabulous. I just can't wait for the election to be over and to see President Donald Trump get to work. All of us get to work. We need new Senators and new House young representatives who love America and are eager to work with our old/new president. I am so excited I just can't hide it. Get the pun?

• Take all the manufacturing out of China, by far our worst enemy. If they thought they could get away with invading Taiwan, they would do it in the blink of an eye. But for now, hold on to your horses, China.

• Just like President Donald Trump said, "Drill, baby, drill." Start drilling the first day in the office. Don't waste any time.

• Rebuild our manufacturing, better than ever. Seventy-five percent of all manufacturing should be made in America. We don't want to be caught with our proverbial pants down. Ever. We should also develop all our electronics and research here.

Let's make the brand "MADE IN AMERICA" famous again.

• Set aside a huge budget for American infrastructure. Millions of Americans will finally have great-paying jobs. But it must happen fast and with great quality

• Let's have our proud farmers work like never before. Make it profitable like before.

• Make our educational system the best ever. Make it number one.

• Change the election system; it's all corrupt. Start new. See Chapter 7. On Elections

• Scrap the health care insurance we have now. It's all corrupt and full of fraud. See Chapter 12. Health Insurance. Fair to everybody. No comprehensive health insurance. It will never be done in our lifetime or ever. One step at a time.

• **AMERICA'S FUTURE IS VERY BRIGHT. Believe in it. Stand up and join hands across America, from sea to shining sea, as the song goes. We will never have a better opportunity like this in a hundred years. Republicans, Democrats, Libertarians, Independents—let's all unite and join this great movement and take our country back. This generation can go down in history as the greatest generation of all time. Don't blink. MAGA forever. Let Us It; AMERICAN RENAISSANCE 2.0**

GOD BLESS THE UNITED STATES OF AMERICA AND ITS PEOPLE

Wendel L. Wilkie, a Republican presidential nominee in 1940, said very proudly: *"I believe in America because we have great dreams and because we have the opportunity to make those dreams come true."*

THE UN

- The United Nations was created after the Second World War. It is an international organization founded in 1945 to cooperate with other nations to promote peace and security. The United States has been sponsoring it since September 14, 1948, in New York.

- The United Nations Charter was intended to play a critical role in promoting stability, security, democracy, human rights, and economic development. It started as a great idea and was relevant for a while, but unfortunately, today it seems to be a collection of mostly socialist politicians who are not able to achieve any of these goals. **ANY GOALS OF THE ABOVE.**

Nowadays, they get involved in matters unrelated to peace and security, such as climate change, poverty, world health, and who knows what else. They are expanding more and more. Who the heck died and put this bunce of ... in charge of all of this? Now there are over 125,000 bureaucrats working for the UN. Are you kidding me? There were less than 1000 employees in 1950, two years after the UN was established in 1948. Now more than 125,000

• The UN today seems to be a very corrupt organization full of thousands of bureaucrats who are just milking the United States of billions of dollars. Many of its member states outright hate the United States and Israel, which should not be acceptable. Countries that grossly violate the human rights of their own people are in charge of human rights. How preposterous is that? **"The fox is in charge of the hen house."** It is so absurd, and if it weren't such a serious matter, it would be laughable. These Countries MUST be forced to make things right or be expelled from the UN.

• Americans have been sponsoring this organization at the rate of (drum roll, please) $18 billion per year. Yes, you read that right: $18 BILLION per year. What do we get for all this money? I'll tell you what; LOTS OF HATE. That's right, lots and lots of hate. Even Canada seems to hate us now. What on earth have we done to Canada to deserve that? They desperately need a new leader. Justin Trudeau, what a clown. How did Canadians elect someone like this? (Don't answer this, it's a trick question. We got President Joe Biden, right?) What, no one else wanted the job? Well, that makes sense. It's their problem. If I were a Canadian, I would start a petition for Canada to become the 51st state of the United States of America. Wouldn't that be grand? We would be the largest country in the world. I would welcome you to America.

• Most of the decisions the UN has made over the last several decades have been against the interests of the United States. And hold on to your pocketbook—they want a lot more money. A LOT MORE. I hope that when President Donald Trump gets into the White House, one of the first things he should do is move the United Nations from New York City to Brussels in the EU. They love politicians there. We've been sponsoring them for 75 years; now let the European Union host them for the next 75 years. Then we'll talk.

• President Donald Trump should push to expel countries that don't respect human rights in their own countries from the UN.

• The United States of America should not pay a penny more per capita than the rest of the member states pay. Let's make it fair.

******* Ginny Brown-Waite (Congresswoman from Florida District 51) on the United Nations: ***The United Nations has***

come under the control of outlaw nations and self-serving special interest groups." I couldn't agree with her more.

REPUBLICANS

John F. Kennedy: *"Let us not seek the Republican answer or the Democratic answer, but the right answer. Let us not seek to fix the blame for the past. Let us accept our own responsibility for the future."* I wish that President Donald Trump would use this quote and a few others from John F. Kennedy. Just saying.

• After Trump wins in November, hopefully with God's help, he will also secure both houses of Congress. Republicans MUST work together as one. Any resistance from any Republican members (most likely a RINO) from either the Senate or House of Representatives MUST be ignored and their power must be completely nullified immediately. They will become just a breathing body among them. The first opportunity, replace him with an America First Believer. MAGA. No more time for games. We must get rid of such individuals, RINOs, as soon as possible, in the first election, no matter what it takes.

• They show us that they are not true patriots. They are NOT willing to pull together in the same direction. They don't want a better America. They are Democrats in Republican clothing, not wanting what all of us WANT. *MAGA*

• This is the biggest opportunity since the inception of the United States. With God's help, we will have Donald Trump as President, who has proven to be the biggest PATRIOT in this country since Abraham Lincoln, bar none.

• If it weren't for him, we would already be a police state by now. Look at what they have done to him since he announced his run for President in 2015. They hit him from all sides and accused him of what Democrats were doing all along. Through investigation in the past 8 years, it was clearly proven that the Democrats (Hillary Clinton herself) were doing everything they accused Trump of doing.

• We must move as one—Republicans and Democrats, Libertarians and Independents—to bring this country back from the depths of ruin brought about by the biggest and meanest American haters and Communists.

• All they care about is staying in power, no matter who is in the White House, and they are willing to do whatever it takes to bring Donald Trump down.

• These super rich people, the Puppet Masters must be exposed and MUST be stopped for what they are. It should truly be illegal for people to give this kind of money to politicians (but this is another chapter—see Chapter 7 on Elections).

Newt Gingrich, 50th speaker of the House of Representatives for 4 years and founder of GOPAC, great PATRIOT said: *"I think one of the great problems we have in the Republican Party is that we don't encourage you to be nasty. We encourage you to be neat, obedient, loyal, and faithful—all those Boy Scout words, which would be great around the campfire, but are lousy in politics."* Yes, he is so right about that.

SLAVERY

Abraham Lincoln's Famous Quote: *This is a world of compensations, and he who would be no slave must consent to have no slave. Those who deny freedom to others, deserve it not for themselves; and, under a just God, cannot long retain it."*

• Slavery has been around for thousands of years. When Countries were at war with each other, the winner would always take all their prisoners and make them slaves.

At the time, the Transatlantic Slave Trade was just getting started, it was the 17th century. The first slaves that were brought to America by the Dutch privateer "The White Lion," brought 20 enslaved Africans to the British Colony of Jamestown, Virginia, in 1619. But that is history now. There were really ugly times. It was very wrong but people in those days were still evolving. It took a man like President

Abraham Lincoln, a Republican I may add who sacrificed his life to make it right. Not just him but thousands of other American Patriots who fought for the slaves' freedom. And they did it. The slaves finally found their freedom. But it was not easy or cheap. Over 600,000 people died, half of them probably fighting for freedom with Abraham Lincoln, for the slaves' freedom. That was a huge sacrifice for America, but it was a sacrifice worth dying for. America was a better Country because of that.

• Why is it that nobody talks about the fact that when President Abraham Lincoln, on January 1, 1863, during the Civil War, wanted to free all the slaves through the "Emancipation Proclamation Edict," every Republican voted YES for it and every single Democrat voted NO for it? Why does no one ask this question?

• That the KKK was founded by the Democrats. That Robert Byrd, a Democrat Senator for over 50 years, was a KKK member.

• That the Democratic machine kept slavery going through the welfare system. Thank you, Lyndon Johnson, for the "War on Poverty" act and the Great Society program. Good intentions, maybe, but bad implementation and a very bad result. More Americans are in poverty now than in 1965. That is a fact.

• Blacks are poorer today than they were before Obama came to power. There are approximately 6 million more people in poverty today than before President Obama's administration. Go figure. People don't want money for nothing; they want a great education and work, RESPECT. They WANT to be in charge of their DESTINY. **See Chapter 8 on Education. This is the truth.**

• Famous Abolitionist and Statesman Frederick Douglass Quote: **"Where justice is denied, where poverty is enforced, where ignorance prevails, and where any one class is made to feel that society is an organized conspiracy to oppress, rob, and degrade them, neither persons nor property will be safe."** Just think about it—where are we today?

RUSSIA

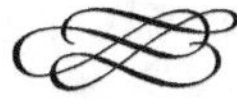

"Russia is a riddle wrapped in a mystery inside an enigma."
The great English Prime Minister Winston Churchill said
about Russia.

• First, regarding the Russian investigation: The politicians
and news media just don't get it. Putin had no interest
whatsoever in having Trump win the presidency. Why
would he? Trump always emphasized "America first," a
strong America, and rebuilding the armed forces stronger
and better than ever. On the other hand, he had Hillary
Clinton in his pocket already—remember the uranium deal?
She was dancing to his tune. She was going to continue
destroying America even further than Obama did, bringing
tyranny to this country and further dismantling the armed
forces. Politicizing and weaponizing all of the top
governmental departments—the State Department, NSA,

IRS, FBI, DOJ, and so on—all to what end? To protect her and further her agenda of moving the country closer to a socialist/communist state or even tyranny. So again, I ask you, if you were Putin, who would you help and hope to become the new American president? A no-brainer, right? Hillary! So where are all those geniuses? Political pundits, news media, and commentators? Why is it that nobody gets it?

Russia vs. Ukraine

• Here is a deal that we can offer President Zelensky and President Putin, which they cannot refuse. No, it's not a horse's head in their bed, Godfather, remember? What I am thinking is the following, and by the way, it's a win-win-win situation. Just follow my reasoning.

Here is the deal:

• To President Zelensky of Ukraine: Stop right now and regain all the territory, including Crimea. With the help of European countries, we will assist Ukraine in rebuilding the country. We will help Ukraine get back all its refugees so they can aid in rebuilding their homeland and create a new, beautiful life at home. This will be possible because we will stop all funding to Ukraine. That is that. So far, so good.

• Now, here comes the real hard and tricky part—making President Vladimir Putin happy. Easier said than done, right? Okay, my deal for President Vladimir Putin would be as follows... Drum roll, please...

Before even starting negotiations, explain to Mr. Vladimir Putin that his biggest enemy is not the United States of America (not at all), the European Union, the United Kingdom, or any other country west or east of them. Their biggest enemy is CHINA. Just think about this: Russia is the largest country in the world, spanning 10 time zones, but with only 144 million people. Russia is just over 17 million square kilometers. A huge area by any standards. That's less than 9 people per square kilometer. Ural and Siberia make up almost 2 thirds of Russia. Most of the eastern part of the country is uninhabited. China could work out a deal with Siberia and Ural by granting them independence from Russia if they (Siberia & Ural) help China to freely traverse their territory and attack Russia by surprise. Siberia and Ural would be all too happy to help. Why not? They would get their independence. Finally. Imagine that, China has 1.5 billion people and over 2 million soldiers. China is a little less than 4 million square kilometers. Just with machine guns, they could overwhelm the Russians. Let alone a full Chinese attack with planes, bombers, rockets, and other military equipment. They would suffocate the Russian army in no time. The Russian army would not stand a chance. Russia can barely keep up with the Ukrainians. The Russian army would collapse within a week. They would lose their country as it is today. Ural and Siberia will get their

Independents and will be gone. Putin and Russia will lose their PRIDE. Russia will never be the same. NEVER. With this said and explained to Mr. Vladimir Putin, I am sure he will get the picture instantly. Now we negotiate:

• He will have to stop the war with Ukraine and immediately withdraw from Ukrainian territory, including Crimea, instantly. They will need to negotiate reparations over a certain number of years for the damages and deaths they caused Ukraine, a certain amount of money.

• They will withdraw from all negotiated treaties with China.

• As a gesture of good faith and trust, Russia will be admitted into NATO as proof that we want to live in peace with them. The United States of America is not the enemy. China definitely is the ENEMY of Russia and America

• This will provide three-fold benefits for the USA:

1. We gained a huge ally.

2. Isolate China from its biggest ally, Russia. Now China is totally isolated from the world, surrounded by enemies on all sides. Let China try to go for Taiwan after this.

3. Bring back to the USA all manufacturing from China, whatever the cost, and bring China to its knees in the process. They will never be a threat to us again, not for a

long, long time. In the process, who knows, Xi Jinping might even lose his grip on power.

• Again, a win-win-win situation. Everybody is happy. Well, not so much China, but they are the ones who got greedy. They gambled and lost.

"You cannot put Russia down on its knees and hold it there because Russia will ultimately pull out."

Mikhail Gorbachev, Russian President in the 80s.

MILITARY SERVICES

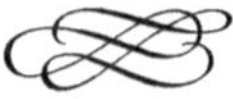

"The greatness of America lies not in being more enlightened than any other nation, but rather in her ability to repair her faults." — Alexis de Tocqueville, a former Deputy of the French National Assembly.

- I believe that all young adults should be required to complete one year of military service. It's about being ready to defend oneself against any threats. They will learn discipline and get in the best shape of their lives.

One year right after high school. They would become a great asset to their own family and to American Security. I wish I could have served for a year in the military. I would. We live in a tumultuous world today and must be prepared for anything. Due to the many unwise politicians we've had over the years, we've made countless enemies.

• In Israel, boys are required to undergo 36 months of military training, while girls have 23 months. So, one year is minimal and does not interfere with school or other important commitments. The world is chaotic, with criminals active in every city. Our children are in grave danger wherever they go. They must learn self-defense.

"I believe our flag is more than just cloth and ink. It is a universally recognized symbol that stands for liberty and freedom. It is the history of our nation, and it's marked by the blood of those who died defending it." John Randolph Thune, a Republican Senator from South Dakota

RONALD REAGAN

President Ronald Reagan said: *"The future doesn't belong to the faint-hearted; it belongs to the brave."* **This is the country of the brave.**

• President Ronald Reagan was one of the best presidents of all time. On the domestic front, Reagan focused on reducing taxes and regulations to stimulate economic growth. He implemented a series of tax cuts, including the Economic Recovery Tax Act of 1981 and the Tax Reform Act of 1986. These measures helped to spur economic growth and create jobs.

• Reagan's presidency was marked by several notable events, including the Iran-Contra affair, which involved secret arms sales to Iran and the diversion of funds to support anti-Sandinista rebels in Nicaragua. This scandal led to the resignation of several high-ranking officials in the Reagan administration, but Reagan himself was not directly implicated.

• Overall, Reagan's presidency had a significant impact on American politics and foreign policy. Ronald Reagan remains a popular figure among many Republicans and conservatives, and his legacy continues to shape political debates in the United States.

• He contributed to the dissolution of the Soviet Union, which brought great joy to hundreds of millions of people across Eastern Europe. Within months, Germany, Yugoslavia, Poland, Romania, Bulgaria, Czechoslovakia, Hungary, and a few other countries all gained their freedom from the USSR.

• Ronald Reagan served as the 40th President of the United States from 1981 to 1989. He was a Republican and is considered one of the most influential and popular presidents of the 20th century. Before his presidency, Reagan was an actor and also served as the Governor of California from 1967 to 1975.

• During his presidency, Reagan focused on several important issues, including foreign policy, domestic policy, and economic policy. He was also well known for his conservative ideology and his efforts to reduce the size of the federal government. Reagan was a strong supporter of the military and played a significant role in bringing the Cold War to an end.

• Reagan's foreign policy was characterized by his belief in the importance of the United States as a global leader. He was well known for his support of the spread of democracy and free markets. Reagan was a strong advocate of the Strategic Defense Initiative (SDI), which aimed to develop a missile defense system designed to protect the United States from nuclear threats. He also played a crucial role in extensive negotiations with Soviet leader Mikhail Gorbachev, which helped reduce tensions between the two superpowers and eventually led to the dissolution of the Soviet Union.

• He was a very good friend of Prime Minister Margaret Thatcher, who was so tough she was called the Iron Lady. Prime Minister Thatcher and President Reagan respected each other greatly. When Argentina decided to take over the Falkland Islands from Great Britain, Ronald Reagan assisted Thatcher in reclaiming the islands in a very short time. They were not only great friends but also great allies.

• All in all, President Ronald Reagan was a great American leader both domestically and internationally. He was one of the best presidents America had until that time.

"When you can't make them see the light, make them feel the heat." The great **Ronald Reagan**